How *Not* to Share Your Faith

MARK BRUMLEY

How *Not* to
Share Your Faith

The Seven Deadly Sins of
Apologetics and Evangelization

CATHOLIC ANSWERS
SAN DIEGO
2002

Published by Catholic Answers, Inc.
2020 Gillespie Way
El Cajon, CA 92020
(888) 291-8000 (orders)
(619) 387-0042 (fax)
www.catholic.com (web)
Cover design by Mary Lou Morreal
Printed in the United States of America
ISBN 1-888992-30-1

Contents

Preface 7

Foreword 11

Introduction 15

1. Apologetical Gluttony 19

2. Reducing the Faith to Apologetics and
   Apologetics to Arguments 31

3. Confusing the Faith with Our Arguments for It 41

4. Contentiousness 49

5. Friendly Fire 59

6. Trying to "Win" 71

7. Pride 81

8. Are the Seven Deadly Sins of Catholic Apologetics
   True Sins? 87

9. What to Do about Them 93

10. Seven Habits of Effective Apologists 97

Conclusion 121

Recommended Reading 123

Preface

The fortunes of apologetics have been volatile indeed. From the sixteenth century to the nineteenth it practically devoured theology. Not only did theologians write books on apologetics; they tended to give an apologetical slant to almost every theological treatise, as though the reasonable person unfailingly could be persuaded to accept what was being taught. The freedom and grace-given character of faith were overlooked; the mysteries of faith were made all too accessible. Especially in liberal Protestantism, the doctrines of the faith were diluted so as to make them credible to supposedly modern men and women.

After the First World War, Karl Barth and others protested against this trend and launched the movement sometimes known as neo-orthodoxy. Revelation, they claimed, must be accepted on its own terms, not on the basis of human arguments. God is not bound to speak and act within the narrow limits of human reason.

Toward the middle of the twentieth century, Barthian influences flowed into Catholicism. Eschewing apologetics, Catholics began to speak the language of neo-orthodoxy. They refused to give reasons for believing. This trend entailed some dangers. Christian belief now began to look like an arbitrary stance—a mere matter of family tradition, personal temperament, or sentiment. Catholics lost interest in challenging others to accept the faith. Evangelization sank to a low ebb. The flow of converts into the Church, which had been vigorous in the first half of the century, slowed down to a trickle.

In the United States, the tradition of Christian apologetics was maintained by Fundamentalists and by many Evangelicals. They insisted that there were solid arguments for accepting Christianity as attested by the Bible and the early creeds. They combined reliance on reason with firm commitment to the central Christian dogmas, such as the Trinity and the Incarnation. They were as

7

orthodox as the neo-orthodox, or rather more so. And their efforts met with considerable success. They sent missionaries all over the world, and as a result their churches grew rapidly, sometimes by converting nominal Catholics to their own brand of Christianity.

Some Catholics in the United States saw this situation as a call to action. This was especially true of Catholics who had a Protestant Evangelical background, such as Peter Kreeft. Recalling that the Catholic Church has a long apologetical tradition of its own, he, together with Karl Keating and a growing body of colleagues, have built fruitfully on the work of English-speaking apologists of the early and mid-twentieth century: Catholics such as G. K. Chesterton and Frank Sheed and Anglicans such as C. S. Lewis. These outstanding writers avoided the pitfalls into which apologists have often fallen. They cannot be accused of tailoring the faith to fit what reason can prove. They knew better than to think that all the mysteries of the faith could be directly proved. And they escaped the "sacred dishonesty" that has prompted some to bend the facts of history so as to conceal the sins and errors of Catholics in the past.

Mark Brumley writes in the spirit of this new Catholic apologetics. He has learned from the failures of liberal Protestantism and from the Barthian critique. Having come to Catholicism as a young adult, he has made the long journey of faith that took him through several Protestant denominations. Married and a father of five, he has worked for some years as a teacher, speaker, and editor.

In writing about the seven deadly sins of apologetics, Brumley is not rejecting apologetics but rather defending it from itself. He shows how an apologetics that seeks to prove too much can undermine the very faith it is intended to support. He also shows how an apologetics that builds on reason alone, instead of deferring to the word of God, can impoverish the faith of Christians, as did liberal Protestantism. In his last chapter he shows how apologetics can be effective when it adheres to the fullness of the faith and respects the primacy of love.

There is no need for me to summarize the contents of this

brief, lively, and eminently readable book. It speaks for itself. The "seven deadly sins" that Brumley identifies are not merely imaginary. Except that kindness restrains him, he could have given blatant examples of each of these vices from authors of the recent past. At a moment when apologetics is gaining new vitality in English-speaking Catholicism, Brumley's book could serve as a valuable handbook for all of the "new apologists." It could save them from the vocational hazards that are almost inseparable from their calling.

— Avery Cardinal Dulles, S.J.
Professor of Religion and Society
Fordham University

Foreword

Go therefore, and make disciples of all nations, baptizing them in the name of the Father and of the Son and of the Holy Spirit, teaching them to observe all that I have commanded you; and lo, I am with you always, to the close of the age [Matt. 28:18-20].

Simple, direct, no-nonsense. These words of Jesus are the greatest mission statement ever written. But in hearing this Scripture so many times in daily life, we can easily become dull to its power. So let's examine it.

First, it is not a suggestion or a request. It is a command. If we say we believe in Jesus Christ, we *must* preach the gospel. We *must* teach the faith, and we must also explain and defend it. There is no Option B. Jesus does not need our polite approval. He does not want our support from the sidelines. He wants us—our love, our zeal, our whole being—because through us he completes the work of salvation, which has never been more urgent for the world than right now.

Second, Jesus is not talking to somebody else. He is talking to you and me. "Go make disciples of all nations" could not be more personal. Jesus wants *you*. The work of evangelizing—and its sibling, apologetics—is not just a job for "professionals." We are the professionals by virtue of our baptism. If the responsibilities of your life prevent you from going to China or Africa, then witness to and defend your faith where you are—to your neighbors, your coworkers, your friends. Find ways to talk about your faith with the people you know. Work to conform your life to the things you say you believe. Make your actions support your words, and your words, your actions.

Third, if Jesus speaks to each of us personally, it is because each of us personally makes a difference. God did not create us by accident. He made us to help him sanctify this world, and to share his joy in the next. The biggest lie of our century is that mass culture is so big and so complicated that an individual cannot make a difference.

This is false. This is the Enemy's propaganda, and we should never believe it. We are *not* powerless. Twelve uneducated Jews turned the Roman world on its head. One Francis Xavier brought tens of thousands of souls to Jesus Christ in the Far East. One Peter Canisius brought tens of thousands of fallen-away Catholics back to the Church.

If Christians were powerless, the world would not feel the need to turn them into martyrs. The gospel has the power to shake the foundations of the world. It has done so many times. It continues to do so today. But it cannot do anything, unless it is lived and preached, taught, explained, and defended. This is why the simplest Christian is the truest and most effective revolutionary. The Christian changes the world by changing one heart at a time.

Fourth, Jesus does not ask the impossible. If he tells us to teach all nations, it is because it can be done. Nothing is impossible with God. When Paul began his work, conversion of the Roman world seemed impossible. But it happened. When Mother Teresa began her work in Calcutta, no one had any idea she would touch people of all nations with her example of Christ's love. But it happened. Do not worry about the odds. They do not concern us. *Never be afraid to speak up for the truth*. God will do the rest.

Fifth, "Go make disciples of all nations" means all nations—the whole world and all its peoples. Jesus is not just "an" answer for some people. Or "the" answer for Western culture. He is not just a teacher like Buddha, or a prophet like Muhammad. He is the Son of God. And what that means is this: Jesus is the answer for every person, in every time, in every nation. There is no other God, and no other Savior. Jesus Christ alone is Lord, and the Catholic Church is the Church he founded. If anyone is saved, he is saved only through Jesus Christ and his Church, whether he knows the name of Jesus or not.

Ecumenical and interreligious dialogues are enormously valuable things. They form us in humility; they deepen our understanding of God; and they teach us respect for our brothers and sisters who don't share our faith but who sometimes radiate Christ's love far better than we do. And yet even our sinfulness does not exempt us from preaching and defending the truth. If we really believe the Catholic faith is the right path to God, then we need to share it joyfully, firmly, with all people and in all seasons. We need to defend it with passion, courage—and also with charity.

The bottom line is this: Our mission is to advance God's work of redeeming and sanctifying the world. Our mission is to bring all people to salvation in Jesus Christ. That is our mission *in community* as the Catholic Church and *individually* as Catholic believers. It's a task of both truth-telling and of love.

The value of Mark Brumley's book is that he helps us see this clearly. He also gives us the tools to act on it. He is articulate, persuasive, balanced, and sensible; and the spirit he brings to this marvelously readable, useful work demonstrates Catholic apologetics at its best: zeal for the truth, informed by patience, respect, and love. I can offer no higher praise.

— Most Rev. Charles J. Chaput, O.F.M. Cap.
Archbishop of Denver

Introduction

Catholic apologetics is back. It is everywhere. Catholic catalogues teem with apologetics books. Apologetics radio and TV programs fill the airwaves. New apologetics apostolates are springing up all over the country—indeed, the world. Surf the Internet and you will find a plethora of apologetics web sites populating cyberspace.

As a convert and an erstwhile professional apologist myself, I see this renaissance as an immensely good thing. In fact, apologetics is an essential part of the Church's evangelical mission, one to which Pope John Paul II constantly refers when, quoting his predecessor, St. Peter, he speaks of believers' duty to "give reasons for the hope" within them (cf. 1 Pet. 3:15). Moreover, the present resurgence of apologetics is a natural result of Vatican II; we should have been deeply worried if the council, as profoundly misunderstood as it has been, had not borne such fruit.

Even so, grave dangers attend the renaissance of apologetics, some so serious that, left unaddressed, they threaten to undermine the good that apologetics can accomplish. (This should not surprise us; the forces of evil always try to pervert the good.) These dangers I call the Seven Deadly Sins of Catholic Apologetics. Like the seven deadly sins of the moral life, they are "deadly" not merely as isolated, individual acts, but as vices, or evil habits —acquired inclinations to act in a certain way.

The seven deadly sins of the moral life are also called the capital sins because they often lead to other sins, not because they are necessarily the worst possible sins. We can say something similar about the Seven Deadly Sins of Catholic Apologetics. They are not necessarily the worst of offenses against authentic Catholic apologetics a person can commit, but they are bad enough, and they tend to lead to other serious "sins" against it.

Sins? Well, let me qualify that. At least one of what I describe as "apologetical sins," pride, *is* sinful, in the ordinary sense of the word: contrary to God's law. But for the most part I use the word *sin* analogously. By it, I mean an action or a tendency to act contrary to the nature and proper end of apologetics. Merely because an apologist errs, for example, in thinking he can prove a certain supernatural mystery from reason alone (Apologetical Gluttony—the First Deadly Sin of Catholic Apologetics) when our affirmation of supernatural mysteries rests on revelation and faith, does not mean he should flee to the confessional or undertake severe mortifications.

I am not speaking of a mere failure of apologetical technique or method. We can argue about the best approach to answering a Jehovah's Witness's questions about the divinity of Jesus Christ. You may prefer to start with John 1:1, while I may start somewhere else. Or you may favor a frontal assault on a doctrinal issue, while I may prefer a more casual, indirect approach. These differences of approach or technique are legitimate. Furthermore, people can be mistaken about which approach to use in any given instance without falling into a "deadly sin" of Catholic apologetics.

Yet the Seven Deadly Sins of Catholic Apologetics are specific acts or bad habits that undercut the apologetical enterprise as such. They can be directly sinful when the action or habit is itself a sin or a tendency toward sinful activities. Or they can be indirectly sinful when they implicate us in sinful behaviors closely tied to them. In that sense, which will be explored in more detail in chapter 8, the sin in the "deadly sins" of Catholic apologetics is not a metaphor.

Whence these "deadly sins"? To the extent they are genuinely sinful, their sources are the world, the flesh, and the devil. But there is a less proximate cause we must consider: an overreaction to widespread misunderstandings and distortions of Vatican II.

For many people, Vatican II did away with the whole business of apologetics. The council, it is rightly said, sought to rid the Church of triumphalism and "to foster whatever can promote union among all who believe in Christ" (*Sacrosanctum Concilium* 1). But many people wrongly conclude that the council was opposed to any kind of apologetic for Catholicism. Thinking ecumenism and apologetics antithetical, many Catholics regard the council's promotion of the one as an implicit repudiation of the other. In fact, if apologetics defends and justifies the faith of the Church in order to help other people to accept that faith, then Vatican II was, among other things, a call to a renewal (not a repudiation) of apologetics. For one way the council sought to "foster whatever can promote union among all who believe in Christ" was "to strengthen whatever can help to call all mankind into the Church's fold" (SC 1). And *that* certainly includes apologetics.

Unfortunately, while trying to correct the imbalance of others' misreading of Vatican II, some Catholic apologists have succumbed to imbalances of their own. This is where the Seven Deadly Sins of Catholic Apologetics come in.

What follows is an exposition of these "deadly sins." This list is certainly not definitive. We could just as easily have settled on nine deadly sins or six deadly sins, adding, subsuming, or subdividing as we wished. The number seven was chosen for the obvious play on the seven deadly sins of the moral life. Even so, the choice of the particular sins in question was not arbitrary. It comes from my experience of over twenty years as an apologist, first as an Evangelical, then as a Catholic. Time and again the seven sins I include here have stood out as being among the most common and dangerous mistakes.

In discussing the Seven Deadly Sins of Catholic Apologetics, I feel a bit like Frank Sheed when he criticized a grave danger to the faith he saw back in the 1960s. The Church suffers, the great apologist and street teacher then observed, in part because Christ has become irrelevant to many Catholics. To them, Christ is, to make reference to the title of one of Sheed's books, "in eclipse." They may identify with him, even pray to him. But they do not really give him much thought in their day-to-day lives. They do not ask themselves what he teaches or allow his doctrine to govern their choices and actions in a serious way.

One Catholic newspaper dubbed this problem "Sheed's disease"—not because Sheed had it but because he had diagnosed it.

That made Sheed wonder whether Parkinson had had Parkinson's disease, for, he admitted, "Sheed certainly has Sheed's disease." Similarly, one reason I can so easily identify the Seven Deadly Sins of Catholic Apologetics is that I have seen and continue to see them all too clearly in my own life.

Apologetical Gluttony

We might call the First Deadly Sin of Catholic Apologetics the Sin of Biting Off More than You Can Chew. Not ordinary gluttony; this is a failure to respect the limits of what apologetics can accomplish. We might also have named this the Deadly Sin of Apologetical Gluttony.

What are the limits of apologetics? Subject matter is one. Some things are beyond the human mind's power to know on its own. Even in the natural order, some mysteries, both scientific and philosophical, are impenetrable by the human mind. And if our knowledge of the natural world is limited, as it seems to be, how much more must be our knowledge of the supernatural order, of God and the things of God?

Unfortunately, some apologists try to prove the unprovable. They forget that apologetics is a branch of sacred theology, which rests on the supernatural mysteries of divine revelation, the word of God, and upon faith. Human reason cannot, on its own power, come to *know* supernatural mysteries; they are above the "natural light of reason." They require *revelation* on God's part and *faith* on ours (cf. *The Catechism of the Catholic Church* 50, 142, 143) if we are going to affirm them.

Proving the Trinity?

We should not pass too quickly over the point. Some knowledgeable apologists agree with it in principle yet do not observe it in practice. For example, an apologist friend once claimed he could prove the doctrine of the Trinity from reason alone, without any appeal to divine revelation. Before he unleashed his argument, I warned him that his success would only lead me to question the Catholic faith. "What do you mean?" he demanded. "Simple," I said. "The Catholic Church holds the dogma of the Trinity to be an article of faith. And articles of faith, on the Catholic view, are beyond unaided reason's ability to prove. Therefore, if you could prove, by reason alone, the dogma of the Trinity—which the Church teaches is an article of faith (cf. CCC 237)—you would succeed in showing the Church right about the Trinity but wrong about faith and reason or what constitutes an article of faith!"

Frank Sheed tells a similar story in his autobiography *The Church and I*. A would-be convert from Hinduism thought he could demonstrate the doctrine of the Trinity. Excited about his insight, he went to Rome, where he was informed that, since the Trinity is a supernatural mystery, it cannot be proved from reason alone. So long as he was convinced it *could* be proved, he was told, he could not be baptized! Unable to abandon his "proof," the man wound up being baptized by a bishop of another church, who, Sheed reports, once declared publicly that the arithmetical aspect of the deity was no concern of his.

It may seem pedantic, but there is a world of difference between truths known on our own power and what we can affirm by faith only. That is why apologists must return again and again to the reality that much of what they do rests on faith and examine whether they argue as if they truly believe it. Vatican I describes faith as "a supernatural virtue whereby, inspired and assisted by the grace of God, we believe that what he has revealed is true, not because the intrinsic truth of things is recognized by the natural light of reason, but because of the authority of God himself who reveals them, who can neither err nor deceive" (*Dei Filius* 3; cf. CCC 155).

John Paul II put it this way in his encyclical *Fides et Ratio*: "By faith, men and women give their assent to the divine testimony. This means that they acknowledge fully and integrally the truth of what is revealed, because it is God himself who is the guarantor of that truth" (13).

Vatican I also distinguished two different ways of coming to the truth, through "natural reason" and through "divine faith":

> [T]here is a twofold order of knowledge, distinct both in principle and in object; in principle, because our knowledge in the one is by natural reason, and in the other, by divine faith; in object, because, besides those things to which natural reason can attain, there are proposed to our belief mysteries hidden in God, which, unless divinely revealed, cannot be known (*Dei Filius* 4; cf. *Gaudium et Spes* 59).

"Faith," wrote Robert Hugh Benson, "is a divine operation wrought in the dark, even though it may seem to be embodied in intellectual arguments and historical facts." On the Catholic view, faith is gratuitous and supernatural; as the work and gift of God, it rests ultimately on his authority, not our arguments. We may *prepare* for it by prayer and by examining the evidence for Catholicism—the signs of credibility indicating that God has spoken or acted here. But faith remains God's gift, wholly above our creaturely intellects' power to generate it. We cannot see the truth of articles of faith as we can see that if A equals B and B equals C then A also equals C. We can resist faith, but we cannot produce it through human effort. Not even the best apologetics argument ever devised can do that.

Here we face what appears, at first glance, to be a contradiction. According to Vatican I,

> in order that the obedience of our faith be nevertheless in harmony with reason (cf. Rom. 12:1), God willed that exterior proofs of his revelation, viz., divine facts, especially miracles and prophecies, should be joined to the interior helps of the Holy Spirit; as they manifestly display the omnipotence and infinite knowledge of God, they are the most certain signs of the divine revelation, adapted to the intelligence of all men. Therefore Moses and the prophets, and especially Christ our Lord himself, performed many manifest miracles and uttered prophecies (*Dei Filius* 3).

Canon 3 of chapter 3 of *Dei Filius* adds, "If anyone says that divine revelation cannot be made credible by outward signs, and that, therefore, men ought to be moved to faith solely by each one's inner experience or by personal inspiration, *anathema sit.*" Canon 4 adds, "If anyone says that no miracles are possible, and that therefore, all accounts of them, even those contained in Holy Scripture, are to be dismissed as fables and myths; or that miracles can never be recognized with certainty, and that the divine origin of the Christian religion cannot be legitimately proved by them, *anathema sit.*"

At the same time, Vatican I teaches that "though the assent of faith is by no means a blind impulse of the mind, still no man can 'assent to the gospel message,' as is necessary to obtain salvation, 'without the illumination and inspiration of the Holy Spirit, who gives to all joy in assenting to the truth and believing it.' " Canon 5 of chapter 3 adds that "if anyone says that the assent to the Christian faith is not free but is produced with necessary arguments of human reason; or that the grace of God is necessary only for that living faith which works by love, *anathema sit.*"

So on the one hand exterior signs, such as miracles, can be proofs of Christian revelation and of the divine origin of Christianity, and on the other, assent to Christian faith cannot be produced "with necessary arguments of human reason." How do we reconcile these seemingly conflicting statements?

Theologians have puzzled over the question for the last hundred years or so. At least part of the solution would seem to hinge on the meaning of the term *external proof.* Miracles are said to be external proofs. In the believer, they are "joined to the interior helps of the Holy Spirit." In other words, miracles can produce "motives of credibility"—indirect proofs that God is acting or revealing himself, or evidence that it is reasonable to believe. But while these may make a man morally certain that he should believe the Christian message or embrace the Catholic Church, they do not by themselves prove the truth of what God has revealed or logically compel the mind's assent to God's word. Simply stated, they do not force us to believe. We do not *see* that what we believe by faith *is* so in the same way we see two and two make four. Arguments may point someone to God's action and even intellectually dispose him to faith, but the grace of faith is still necessary if someone is to believe.

There is far more to the question than that, as theologians would be quick to note. But at least this helps explain why intelligent people can listen to well-constructed arguments for the faith and still not believe. It remains possible for a man to reject the grace of faith, notwithstanding the rational force of arguments. Arguments can lead us to conclude that God has revealed himself in such and such a way. They can even be morally convincing. And yet they are not so straightforward and compelling that the intellect is forced to accept them, so in that sense, arguments do not directly prove the truth of the Catholic faith. God's word must still be accepted by faith.

Nor is the necessity of faith a consequence of the fall. Traditional theology holds that even if the human intellect were unaffected by sin, faith would be necessary in order to affirm a supernatural mystery, strictly defined. Why? Because supernatural mysteries are beyond the power of any created nature to know. Not even the unfallen angels, with their towering intellects, can penetrate the truth of a strictly supernatural mystery by their natural powers. But human beings have an additional problem when it comes to knowing such truths: the darkening of the human intellect as a result of the fall.

To be sure, Catholicism rejects the view of some that the intellect's power to know religious truth apart from revelation is utterly corrupted. We can, for instance, come to know that God exists and that there is a moral order, apart from divine revelation.[1] We can even examine the various signs of credibility and

---

[1] According to St. Thomas Aquinas, the existence of God is not an article of faith *as such* but a preamble to faith (*Summa Theologiae* I:2:2, rep. obj. 1). This is because God's existence can be known apart from revelation and faith. Only for those who, for whatever reason, cannot come to the knowledge of God's existence from reason apart from faith is it an article of faith. Furthermore,

reach probable conclusions about God's action in human history. But doing all of this can be difficult, and we remain prone to error and to getting lost in obscurity. This, too, is why God has revealed himself and why he moves man, by the grace of faith, to believe. The apologist who overlooks the darkening of the human intellect will mistakenly treat those with whom he dialogues as if their human natures were unfallen. But more on that later.

The Will to Believe

The mysteries of faith limit what apologetics can accomplish with the human intellect. They also limit what we can do with the human will. Some apologists mistakenly think that sound, cogent arguments will inevitably compel faith in an intelligent person by inducing the human will to force the intellect to believe. A story about the philosopher Mortimer Adler illustrates this error. Clare Boothe Luce, a famous convert to the Catholic faith, once asked Adler why he, who had rigorously studied the philosophy and theology of St. Thomas Aquinas, had not become a Catholic. He replied that his state of mind was much closer to what St. Thomas called "dead faith" than "living faith"—dead faith being faith without charity. Later, he realized his answer was inadequate. In his autobiography *Philosopher at Large*, published in 1977, he wrote more candidly:

> The only reason to adopt a religion is that one wishes and intends to live henceforth in accordance with its precepts, forswearing conduct and habits that are incompatible. For me to become a Roman Catholic—or, for that matter, an Anglo-Catholic or Episcopalian —would require a radical change in my way of life, a basic alteration in the direction of my day-to-day choices as well as in the ultimate objectives to be sought or hoped for. I have too clear and too detailed an understanding of moral theology to fool myself on

---

human beings can know fundamental moral truths from the natural law, which is knowable by means of natural reason without revelation and faith.

that score. The simple truth of the matter is that I did not wish to live up to being a genuinely religious person. I could not bring myself to will what I ought to will for my whole future if I were to resolve my will, at a particular moment, with regard to religious conversion (316).

Seldom do nonbelievers put it so honestly. Thanks be to God, in 1984, Adler became a Christian, taking the leap of faith, going from being a person who merely affirmed the existence of God —the God of the philosophers—to one who believed and loved God. (The story of his conversion to Christianity is recounted in *A Second Look in the Rearview Mirror: Further Autobiographical Reflections of a Philosopher at Large*, in the chapter called "A Philosopher's Religious Faith." This book is a sequel to Adler's *Philosopher at Large*.) In 2000, a year before his death, Adler was received into the Catholic Church, thus completing—from the Catholic point of view—the journey to faith he began when he became a Christian.

The Adler story underscores a limit the human will places on what apologetics can achieve: no matter how good an argument we offer someone or how good a grasp of Catholicism that person may have, he can still say no to grace and, hence, not come to faith. To think otherwise is tacitly to embrace the Calvinist notion of the irresistibility of grace, or, worse still, the idea that apologetics works by the force of our syllogisms rather than by conversion and the movement of the Holy Spirit.

Summarizing the First Two Limits

Catholic teaching stresses what at times may seem to be two contradictory aspects of the act of faith. First, man is incapable of believing on his own, apart from God's grace; second, faith is not compelled but free.

On the first point, Vatican II's Constitution on Divine Revelation, *Dei Verbum*, states that before man can believe, he "must have the grace of God to move and assist him; he must have the

interior helps of the Holy Spirit, who moves the heart and converts it to God" (5). At the same time, "The act of faith is of its
very nature a free act," as Vatican II's Declaration on Religious
Liberty, *Dignitatis Humanae*, reminds us (10). Not even God co-
erces man to believe: "God calls men to serve him in spirit and
in truth. Consequently, they are bound to him in conscience but
not coerced. God has regard for the dignity of the human person
which he himself created; the human person is to be guided by
his own judgment and to enjoy freedom" (DH 11).

Here, however, these aspects of faith reinforce the point about
the limits of what apologetics can do. When the apologist sets out
to defend an article of faith, the best he can hope to accomplish
with an unbeliever is to show that the doctrine in question does
not contradict reason and that there is evidence that God has revealed the truth in question. The former shows that the doctrine
can reasonably be believed, while the latter shows that it *should*
be believed. After all, if God has revealed something, we should
believe it, even though we cannot see how it is so. But the apologist cannot simply argue the unbeliever into believing or generate
the act of believing, because the apologist cannot compel God's
grace to act on that person's will or mind, which is necessary for
the act of faith to occur. Nor can the apologist force the man to
cooperate with grace, should God act on his heart to move him
to believe. The unbeliever remains free to say no.

The Limit of Feelings

A third element of the human situation as we experience it can
limit our reception of the truth—feelings. For some people, feelings pose the greatest obstacle to embracing Catholicism. By *feelings* I mean our attitudes, our likes and dislikes, the residue of
our upbringing and experience. Feelings often color our thinking
and choosing so that an otherwise rational person, disposed to
choose the good, cannot see in a particular instance what truly is
good. He may find himself unable to choose it even if he knows

or suspects what it is. In this way, feelings can inhibit our minds and restrict our freedom to choose and to act.

Consider an extreme example: a Polish-Jewish Holocaust survivor whose family was betrayed, let us say, by Christian neighbors. He remembers years of Christian anti-Semitism that occurred long before Hitler invaded Poland or the Nazis deported him and his family to a concentration camp. He recalls being taunted as a "Christ killer" by Christian children. He remembers Christians standing by as his fellow Jews disappeared. Then he remembers the betrayal, how his Christian neighbors denounced his father, his mother, his brothers, and himself to the Nazis—and how he alone survived the death camps.

Is it really surprising that such a man would have difficulty analyzing arguments for and against Christianity or Catholicism with rational detachment? That is not to say that, by God's grace, such a thing could not happen, only that the emotions generated by such a horrendous experience as the Holocaust can affect how people perceive apologetical arguments.

Nor does it take an event as traumatic as the Holocaust to create emotional or psychological obstacles to Catholicism. In his book *C. S. Lewis and the Church of Rome*, the English Catholic writer Christopher Derrick argues that Lewis's Ulster Protestant upbringing had much to do with why the great Christian apologist never became a Catholic. Derrick was a student and friend of Lewis, and others who knew Lewis have said the same thing. If childhood prejudices can inhibit the rational processes of a great mind such as that of C. S. Lewis, then surely they can create problems for ordinary intellects.

Thus we should not minimize the effects of feelings and experiences on our power to perceive and accept the truth. Sometimes apologists argue away, as if those with whom they argue will always respond like *Star Trek*'s Mr. Spock, with unemotional, rational objectivity. But, like it or not, feelings matter.

The Two Dimensions of Apologetics

Apologetics, we should always remember, has its objective and subjective aspects. The objective case for Catholicism includes arguments pointing to signs of God's work in history. These are motives for belief. The person who recognizes the credibility of the gospel as presented by the Catholic Church is obliged in conscience to embrace it. There are, however, certain human needs —real needs as opposed to mere preferences or desires—that only God can satisfy. Once a man believes God satisfies his needs fully only in the Catholic Church, he will be inclined to embrace it. This is the subjective aspect to apologetics, subjective because it emphasizes the perceived needs of the subject rather than the objective truth of the Catholic faith.

Obviously the two aspects are related to each other. The objective reality of Catholicism corresponds with the subjective needs of human beings, whether they perceive those needs accurately or not. Furthermore, these two aspects of apologetics have their respective methods, objective and subjective.

In his book *Now I See*, Arnold Lunn summarized well the objective method of apologetics:

> It is no use imploring people to try the Christian way of life until you have convinced them that Christianity is true. The attractions of this way of life are not self-evident. The Christian way of life is a way of self-denial and self-discipline, which are worthwhile if, and only if, Christianity is true. The first duty of the evangelist, therefore, is to prove that Christianity *is* true (16).

The stress in the objective method is on demonstrating the objective truth of Catholicism. Little regard is given to the subjectivity of the audience.

The subjective method takes a different tack, recognizing that many people will not consider the truth of a religion unless they see its relevance to their lives, to what they perceive to be their needs as human beings. If Christianity in general or Catholic Christianity in particular can be shown to satisfy man's deepest longings, people are more apt to consider its truth claims and to embrace it.

In the nineteenth century and throughout the better part of the twentieth, most apologists and theologians stressed the objective aspect of apologetics. They would make the rational case for Christianity or Catholic Christianity, on objective grounds, then challenge people to examine that case. There were exceptions to this tendency—the French Catholic philosopher Maurice Blondel, for example. But by and large the objective method in apologetics dominated the theological scene.

In the 1950s and 1960s, and especially immediately after Vatican II, some theologians began to stress the subjective dimension of apologetics, among them the German theologian Karl Rahner, and those who belonged to the so-called school of Transcendental Thomism. Some people considered the objective approach to apologetics to have been discredited. For others, it was a question of which of the two aspects should be stressed in the present age, with its emphasis on the subject and on the individual's perception of things rather than on whether one or the other aspect of apologetics is false or less true in itself. Some theologians, such as Hans Urs von Balthasar, sought to integrate elements of the two approaches to theology and apologetics. But for the most part, the objective approach to apologetics fell into disfavor.

Fundamentalist and other attacks on Catholicism from the 1970s through the 1990s led to a recovery of the objective aspect of apologetics and, correspondingly, a more objective method. For the most part, "the New Apologetics," as it has been called, stresses the objective dimension. In an age of widespread relativism and skepticism, subjective apologetics can easily become subjectivism. The objective aspect of apologetics provides a necessary balance.

Even so, Catholic apologists should take care not to ignore the subjective dimension. Otherwise apologetics appears not to respond to the real demands of the human heart. Faith can then seem an abstraction, a distant syllogism rather than a vital reality, a saving union with the one who said, "I am the way, and the truth, and the life" (John 14:6). Catholicism may well be true, but what of it? What does it mean for *me*? The challenge for twenty-first-century Catholic apologists is to maintain a balance, to integrate both the objective and the subjective dimensions of apologetics.

Apologetical Anorexia

The human mind, will, and feelings, then, limit what apologetics can accomplish. After all, when we believe, it is the whole man who believes, not merely an intellect or a will. Mind, will, and feelings limit the subject, man, and this particular subject, Jack, with his personal weaknesses, tendencies of thought, and experiences. The First Deadly Sin of Catholic apologetics is to ignore all of this and blithely engage in apologetics as if nothing were impossible to the knowledgeable, articulate apologist with his arsenal of proofs and arguments. Such an attitude exemplifies Apologetical Gluttony, the result of which can be apologetical indigestion, in which the apologist finds his work less nourishing to the spirit than it ought to be. It can also lead to disappointment and even, by way of overreaction, to a kind of fideism that despairs of theological argument altogether. You might call it a sort of apologetical anorexia, in which the failures of a once overconfident apologist lead to sheer agnosticism about apologetics and human reason. In its extreme form, it can even lead to apostasy, leaving the apologist not only ineffectual but bereft of faith itself.

2

Reducing the Faith to Apologetics
and Apologetics to Arguments

"It is absurd to argue men, as to torture them, into believing," said Newman. From this comment, many Christians wrongly conclude that there is no point at all in arguing about religion. "Argument never convinced anyone," they say.

Not so. To reply that an argument against arguments is illogical and self-refuting might seem sophistry to the anti-intellectual or the fideist. What cannot be gainsaid, by either one, are facts. It is a fact that people change their minds all the time as a result of arguments.

Catholic apologists, therefore, should not apologize for arguing about the faith. What we must not do is exaggerate the place of argument—understood here as presenting the rational case for something—in Christian faith or even in apologetics as such. Argument poses serious temptations for apologists. In fact, the Second Deadly Sin of Catholic Apologetics might be called *Reductio ad Apologeticum et Argumentum*, Reducing Everything to Apologetics and Argument. By *everything* I mean the Christian life as a whole. The error here is in looking at all or most spiritual matters "apologetically." When your only tool is a hammer, as the saying goes, you tend to approach everything as if it were a nail. When apologetics becomes your only tool for understanding Christianity, and argument the only tool for engaging in apologetics, you may try to nail all theological and spiritual subjects with apologetical arguments or put them into an apologetical category.

Consider a real-life example. A Catholic apologist friend once told me how during the sacred liturgy he routinely thought up arguments to defend the Real Presence. At first, they just popped into his head, he said. Then he began to cultivate them, to try to think them up at Mass. What is more, my friend did not see any problem with doing this. He looked forward to Mass because, he said, it was such fertile ground for apologetics arguments.

Now it is fine to meditate on the Real Presence at Mass. It may even, on occasion, be legitimate to think about arguments in defense of the Real Presence at Mass. But surely we risk neglecting the spiritual communion we are invited to have with God and neighbor, and the divine worship we are obliged to offer God, if the sacred liturgy is reduced to a debate-prepping session. At Mass, we are called not merely to *think* about Jesus or contemplate arguments to support the doctrine of his Real Presence, but to *give* ourselves to the Father through the Son in the Holy Spirit. We are called to *receive* the eucharistic Christ and to become one with him and with the rest of his body, the Church. To focus on creating and analyzing arguments about him at Mass misses the point. It confuses ends with means.

Some people become so hooked on apologetical arguments that they forget apologetics is a *means* to the end of believing God's word; it should not become the goal. Furthermore, simply because we argue well or make converts does not mean we are personally "right with God"—which is what being a Catholic is about. Frank Sheed once told of a Catholic Evidence Guild speaker who later revealed that while he had been lecturing for the guild, he secretly kept a mistress. That the man was living in sin, Sheed noted, did not detract from the power of the truth he proclaimed. On the other hand, the fact that the man's message converted hearts did not absolve him of sin. It may well have deepened his culpability.

Bad Spirituality Leads to Bad Apologetics

Similarly, our ability to marshal arguments for Catholic doctrine will not save us. If those who say, "Lord, did we not work miracles in your name? Did we not cast out demons in your name?" (cf. Matt. 7:22), can be damned, we should not think, "Did we not make converts in your name? Did we not fashion the best apologetics arguments?" will get us far. Indeed, the more we know, the higher the standard by which we will be judged. "To whom much is given," Jesus says, "much will be required" (cf. Luke 12:48).

A general spiritual danger all Christians face, which can become more acute for the apologist (not to mention the theologian), is that of missing the point of the Catholic faith. St. Paul feared preaching to others but being lost himself and, therefore, took steps to avoid it; the apologist should, too. The point of the Catholic faith is not to argue or even to make converts. It is to know and love God. Of course one way the apologist knows and loves God is by arguing for his truth and trying to make converts. Yet we can manage to do those things for other, less appropriate reasons.

Because the apologist, whether professionally or as an avid amateur, is immersed in the doctrine of the faith, he can mistake his work for the Christian life itself. He can think he lives the faith merely because he argues for it, that he is growing in charity merely because he loves to refute error. But God will play second fiddle to nothing, not even to apologetics. God wants the apologist's heart as well as his mind, and he wants his mind for more than devising arguments.

The apologist's faith, then, must be genuine, not merely the holding of certain propositions to be true. It must also be faith "formed" by charity. He must not only submit to God by believing what God says is true, but submit in charity, too, loving God above all things for God's own sake, and loving his neighbor as himself. This applies to all Christians, of course, but the intellectual nature of what apologists do puts them at special risk in this area. We shall return in chapter 10 to the subject of apologists and charity.

Besides being bad spirituality, the reduction of Catholicism to apologetics is also bad apologetics. We can defend the faith or show its credibility in other ways besides rational argument. Sheed once made the point that the apologist appeals to the intellect; the preacher, to the will. That is true, but the intellect can be appealed to in other ways besides logic (yes, Mr. Spock, there is more to the life of the mind than logic).

Catholicism often captivates people by its goodness and beauty, as well as by its logical truth. Many people's objections to the faith are overcome in ways some apologists completely ignore: through art rather than arguments, through sanctity rather than syllogisms. This man discovers the beauty of the liturgy or the goodness of the saints, and his objections to God evaporate. That woman captures (or is captured by) the Catholic vision through a Catholic novel, a cathedral, a painting. Suddenly, she sees her need for faith and turns to God. Someone else is impressed by the witness of an ordinary, committed Catholic life. By reducing the case for Catholicism to rational arguments, the misguided apologist neglects many things that bring people to faith or help them overcome objections to it.

In many ways, what we need today is an aesthetical apologetic or an apologetical aesthetic, to complement (but not negate) other kinds of apologetics activities, which tend to be heavily logical or rationalist. Fr. Thomas Dubay has written about the "evidential power of beauty"—that is, its power to lead people to truth. He stresses how modern science has begun to discover beauty as a means of devising sound theories about the universe. Scientists must still confirm their theories by experiment, of course, but beauty seems to help point them in the right direction. As Fr. Dubay notes, the Nobel prize-winning physicist Richard Feynman once observed, "You can recognize truth by its beauty and simplicity." Catholic apologists would benefit from applying that maxim to their work.

Hans Urs von Balthasar pioneered the theological foundations of an aesthetical apologetics. He wrote of a theological aesthetic, *The Glory of the Lord*, the idea behind which was "seeing the form" of the faith, finding the truth manifest in its beauty. Von Balthasar was concerned with theology in general, but it is just one step from that to an apologetical aesthetic or an aesthetical apologetics (whichever way you want to put it).

Much of what goes on in apologetical exchange, it seems to me, amounts to helping non-Catholics see the world, God, or Christianity with Catholic eyes. The trouble is, we sometimes think we have won people over by the sheer logical force of argument. There are impediments to seeing the Catholic form, and the apologist, as a kind of ophthalmologist of faith, can sometimes remove them. There may even be personal difficulties affecting one's vision—theological myopia, which the apologist can help correct as an eye doctor may use eyeglasses or laser surgery. In the final analysis, though, the apologist cannot bestow vision on his patient; only God can do that by providing the light of faith.

Related to an aesthetical apologetics is what we could call an apologetics of holiness in which the beauty of holiness works to overcome objections to faith. Since, as we have seen, there is a link between beauty and truth, many people become convinced of Catholicism's truth through the witness of holiness. When non-Catholics look at the lives of Catholic saints, they are often drawn toward the Church. The saints are, after all, models of discipleship and holiness. The Protestant, for instance, who seriously desires to be Jesus' disciple, will notice the fruit Catholicism has borne in the lives of the saints. This may move him to consider Catholic claims. As Pope Paul VI said, "Modern man listens more willingly to witnesses than to teachers, and if he does listen to teachers, it is because they are witnesses" (*Evangelii Nuntiandi* 41). The saints are holy witnesses to the truth of the Catholic faith.

Finally, let me mention here another indirect form of apologetics, the apologetics of secular competence. That, at least, is my name for it. C. S. Lewis described the kind of thing I mean, in his essay "Christian Apologetics." Lewis argued that a Christian who can write a good popular work on science, let us say, may be more effective than one who writes a directly apologetic work. By that he did not mean that a Christian should slant his account of science to favor the faith; he dismissed such an idea as "sin and folly." Lewis envisioned a situation in which, whenever the average man wanted a readable introduction to a subject, he would find that the best book in the field was written by a Christian. The Christianity of the work would be latent, and the book would be completely honest to its subject matter. Nevertheless, the Christian worldview would shine through. Reading it, the non-Christian would begin to wonder whether his secular, anti-Christian presuppositions were right after all. "Perhaps there *is* something to Christianity," he might think.

As Catholics, we can agree wholeheartedly with Lewis and go him one better. Certainly it would be a potent statement about the Catholic faith if the best secular books on, say, science, history, politics, or economics were written by Catholics and permeated, latently, of course, with the Catholic ethos. But it would also be a powerful witness if the best religious books, including the best apologetic works for Christianity in general, were written by Catholics. That, of course, would take things beyond the apologetics of secular competence to an indirect apologetic for Catholicism over against other brands of Christianity. But the idea of indirection remains. The immediate purpose would be to explain and defend theism or Christianity; the indirect effect would be to lead non-Catholics—non-Christian and Christian—to consider Catholicism.

As an Evangelical Christian, I was attracted to the Catholic Church, in part, because of the potent *Christian* apologetics of people like G. K. Chesterton and Frank Sheed. Their arguments for Christianity, as distinct from any arguments they made for the Catholic Church, led me to ponder how such evidently intelligent and good men could buy into Catholicism. "Perhaps there is something to this Catholic thing," I thought.

For if the Catholic Church possesses the fullness of Christianity, her primary business should be to point people not to herself as such, but to Jesus Christ. Indeed, the Church directs people toward herself only because she is the body and spouse of Jesus, who is Head and Bridegroom of the Church; she does not stand as an independent spiritual good over against Jesus Christ. The Church is the sacrament of salvation because she is the sacrament of Jesus. Vatican II says the Church is a kind of sacrament (*Lumen Gentium* 1), but it qualifies that with the words "in Christ." The Church is, "in Christ, a kind of sacrament—a sign and instrument of communion with God and of the unity of the human race." By presenting the Catholic Church as every bit as eager as Evangelical churches to bring people to Jesus Christ, if not more so, Catholic apologists indirectly witness to the truth of the Catholic faith.

You see, in the back of many Evangelical minds lurks a dark suspicion: Catholics care more about the Church than about Jesus Christ. Catholic apologists play no small part in fostering this myth if they give the impression that they think believing in Jesus is fine enough but that the really important thing is belonging to the Catholic Church. But the two are not really separable, though we can distinguish them at the visible level of actual church affiliation. The person who is truly joined to Jesus Christ is, according to Catholic teaching, truly joined to the Catholic Church whether he realizes it or not. He may not be in full communion with the Catholic Church, but he is at least in imperfect (yet real) communion with her. That is why people who are not formally members of the Catholic Church—those who have not been, as Vatican II says, "fully incorporated" into the Church—can nonetheless be saved, even though the Catholic Church maintains that "outside the Church there is no salvation."

The goal, then, is to help the non-Catholic to see that everything said of the Catholic Church is said because of the Church's relationship with Jesus. Christ continues to act in and through the community of his disciples, the Church. Thus, to do justice to Jesus Christ, we must speak as well about his Church. But it is Jesus who concerns us first and foremost. Evangelical Christians are right to see the centrality of Jesus as the touchstone of genuine apologetics and, more broadly, of Christian truth. Focusing on Jesus Christ in Catholic apologetics is a good strategy because it happens to correspond to the real mission of the Church!

The Insufficiency of Scripture

The *reductio ad argumentum* of Catholic apologetics sometimes takes the form of proof-texting, the practice of trying to prove a certain doctrine by citing a series of texts. This is especially true when it comes to arguing with other Christians or quasi-Christian groups. Is there a dispute over whether Jesus is God? Well, pull together some Bible verses and settle the matter. John 1:1 says, "In the beginning was the Word, and the Word was with God, and the Word was God." John 1:14 tells us, "The Word became flesh and dwelt among us." When the risen Jesus appears to doubting Thomas, Thomas declares, "My Lord and my God!" (John 20:28). And so on.

Obviously, using the Bible to make a case for Catholic doctrine can be very powerful with someone who accepts the authority of the Bible. That many Catholics today know the Bible well enough to use it to defend their faith is an extraordinarily good thing. All the same, it is sometimes best simply to present the doctrine, without proof-texts, even without argument, and let its power to attract work. Why? Because some people today are indifferent to proofs and logical arguments, especially when it comes to religion.

Back in the 1940s, Frank Sheed made the same point (in the introduction to his *Catholic Evidence Guild Outlines*). "Proof," he wrote, "for the present day Catholic apologist, has gone into comparative eclipse." In its place, Sheed proposed exposition of doctrine—sheer presentation, in as intelligible a fashion as possible, of what the Church believes, what she sees when she reads Scripture, and what it means. The modern street-corner apologist, Sheed contended, ought to devote nine-tenths of his effort to explaining what a doctrine is and why it is important, and only one-tenth to proving it. From my own experience as an apologist, it seems to me that Sheed was on to something that remains relevant today.

Let me add that I have come to this conclusion after much personal struggle, and I offer it with one sizable proviso. When someone has a real objection to the faith based on a text or texts, as many Evangelical Protestants do, it is not good to duck the question. In other words, when I say it is "sometimes best simply to present the doctrine and let its power to attract work," rather than to cite proof-texts, I mean *sometimes*, not *always*. One of the blessings of the new apologetics movement is the wonderful recovery and use of the Bible. In no sense do I intend to demean that or to leave the impression that apologists should not be aware of the most helpful biblical texts or know how to use the Bible to answer objections raised against the faith. One of the big problems we have today is that the typical Catholic priest or deacon, not to mention the ordinary layman, does not know the Bible well enough to defend the faith.

We can rely too much on particular texts, however, with the result that the person we are discussing the faith with gets lost in a stream of biblical citations. Very soon an exchange over a biblical text can degenerate into a contest of dueling Bibles, with this text countering that, and so on. In the process, it is easy to lose the big picture.

Besides, sometimes there simply is no proof-text to support a particular point. Where, for example, do we find a text saying that Mary was assumed bodily into heaven? Of course the overall biblical witness supports the bodily Assumption of the Blessed Virgin—*pace* many Fundamentalist critics, the doctrine was not concocted out of thin air or pious legend. But "seeing the biblical form" requires more than tramping through a series of verses. It requires the ability to understand the doctrine in the panoramic context of salvation history, to see the relationship of Christ to Adam, of Mary to Christ, and of Mary to Eve, not to mention the eschatological dimension of Mary's position as the type of the Church.

Almost all apologists I know who make biblical arguments for the Blessed Mother's Assumption accept the need for communicating that panoramic view. Yet some apologists mistakenly think that doing so amounts to a biblically and logically airtight argument for the Assumption. That mistake only serves to reinforce a false idea under which some apologists labor: that the case for Catholic doctrine is nothing more than logical conclusions to arguments drawn from a series of proof-texts.

To be sure, sometimes a sound argument can be based on the Bible. The Jehovah's Witnesses' view of Jesus, for example, can be disposed of by careful, step-by-step reasoning through certain biblical texts. But a sound argument is not always a convincing one. The person with whom you argue will not necessarily be convinced by your argument, however well framed it may be. Some former Jehovah's Witnesses say they were more convinced of the divinity of Jesus by the personal relationship their Christian dialogue partner had with him than by any particular biblical text or set of texts. Of course, that is not an argument against arguments—an absurdity, as we have said—but an argument for recognizing their limits.

3

Confusing the Faith with Our Arguments for It

The Third Deadly Sin of Catholic Apologetics is to confuse the faith with *our* arguments for it. It is not simply a matter of reducing the Catholic faith to the arguments, but of reducing the faith to our own *particular* arguments for it, or at least to those particular arguments we find useful or persuasive. One danger there should be obvious: when our argument falters, so might our faith. C. S. Lewis put the point well in an essay on Christian apologetics:

> I have found that there is nothing more dangerous to one's own faith than the work of an apologist. No doctrine of that faith seems to me so spectral, so unreal as one that I have just successfully defended in a public debate. For a moment, you see, it has seemed to rest on oneself: as a result, when you go away from that debate, it seems no stronger than that weak pillar. That is why we apologists take our lives in our hands and can be saved only by falling back continually from the web of our own arguments, as from our intellectual counters, into the reality—from Christian apologetics into Christ himself (*God in the Dock* 103).

Lewis's statement also applies to Catholic apologists. Our faith should be made of sturdier stuff than the particular arguments we contrive to defend it. Furthermore, merely because we fail in argument and do not actually demonstrate what we set out to prove does not mean the thing we argued for is false. Yet if we ally our faith too closely with our arguments, the fate of the one will seem to guarantee the fate of the other.

The Special Susceptibility of Converts

When it comes to confusing our arguments for the faith with the faith they are devised to defend, we converts from Evangelicalism are especially susceptible. Many of us argued ourselves into the Catholic Church, doctrine by doctrine. Often we reluctantly embraced, say, transubstantiation or the Assumption of the Blessed Virgin Mary against the beliefs of dear brothers and sisters of our own church or denomination—perhaps even against those of a spouse. But we arrived at these truths differently from the typical Catholic, who starts with the faith of the Church rather than by paging through the Bible to discover what to believe. As Evangelicals, we regarded these hard-won theological truths as, in a certain sense, our discoveries or our interpretations of the Bible, even when we humbly adopted them. The danger is that even after becoming Catholics, some converts may still (perhaps unconsciously) regard certain doctrines as their own.

I have known new converts, especially from Evangelicalism and Fundamentalism, to fall into this trap. So tenaciously do they cling to particular doctrines as their personal discoveries, that they sometimes think they can teach the Church a thing or two about Catholic truth. When their approaches to particular doctrines are not immediately applauded by Church authority, they are tempted to judge even the Magisterium to be less truly Catholic than they are. Zeal for their own arguments supplants the docility proper to a follower of Christ and member of his Church.

One former Evangelical I know was greatly influenced by the Church's teaching against contraception and divorce and remarriage. Since most Protestant denominations allow contraception and, at least under some circumstances, divorce and remarriage of Christians, he was not initially receptive to Catholic teaching in these areas. He saw it as another example of what he called "Catholic totalitarianism," what he regarded as a tendency of the Church to try to control all areas of the lives of her members.

After careful, prayerful study of Scripture and Christian history, my friend changed his mind. He became convinced that contraception and divorce and remarriage are always contrary to God's will. And he was fascinated by the fact that the Catholic Church alone among historic Christian bodies has held fast on these points. That persuaded him to consider Catholic teaching in other areas and eventually led to his reception into the Catholic Church.

"Praise the Lord!" you may say to yourself, and of course I agree with the sentiment. Unfortunately, the story does not end there. So obsessed was my friend with the issues of contraception and divorce and remarriage, and so convinced was he of his own arguments on the subject, that he quickly found himself at odds with the Church. You see, his particular approach to the issue of contraception led him to reject all forms of family planning, including natural family planning (NFP), as essentially contraceptive. He became convinced that NFP is an erroneous concession to the antichild, antiprovidential mentality of the modern world.

Ironically, my friend agrees with many proponents of contraception that since both users of NFP and contraceptives have the same end in view, avoidance of pregnancy, the means to achieve that end must be morally equivalent. He is completely unfazed by the standard pro-NFP rejoinder: having the same end in view does not make the means of attaining the end morally equivalent. You can support your family by honest work or by robbing convenience stores. Merely because the end, supporting your family, is the same in both cases does not mean that labor is morally equivalent to theft. Likewise with NFP and contraception. That both can be used to avoid pregnancy does not make them morally equivalent. But my friend will not—or cannot—see the distinction, at least not in terms of his own arguments against contraception.

Let me be clear. Many writers have suggested that couples using NFP should regularly examine their motives for doing so. Have they allowed an antichild, contraceptive mentality to influence their practice of NFP? But my friend objects to NFP in principle, not only in how it is practiced: he does not think it is morally permissible to practice NFP under any circumstances because it violates Catholic tradition as well as the natural law.

My friend's view of NFP puts him at odds with the teaching of *Humanae Vitae*, which distinguishes NFP from contraception. Catholics, according to *Humanae Vitae* (and the encyclical of Pope Pius XI, *Casti Connubii*), may licitly use NFP if they have sufficient reasons. But under no circumstances may they contracept, even with the best of intentions.

My friend also has a problem with the Catholic Church's teaching on annulments. It is not simply that there are too many annulments today—who can argue against that? Nor is it merely a question of whether tribunals are declaring a large number of unions null that are actually valid—which is a different proposition and a debatable one. No, he rejects the very idea of annulment, seeing it as a concession to the divorce-and-remarriage mentality. "Once again," he argues, "the Catholic Church has caved in to the spirit of the world, although less gravely than Protestantism and Orthodoxy."

Where does this leave the former Evangelical now? Almost out of the Catholic Church. His problems with Catholic teaching on NFP and annulments have led him to reevaluate other aspects of Catholic doctrine, including Vatican II. He now regards as heretical Vatican II's teaching on the possibility of salvation for non-Catholics in good faith. And since Popes John XXIII and Paul VI approved the council and Paul VI promulgated its documents, my friend also questions whether they, in fact, were legitimate holders of the papal office. He is sympathetic to sedevacantism, the view that the putative pope is invalid and that the papal office is now vacant.

My Arguments vs. the Faith

Theologians sometimes distinguish doctrines *about* Christ and the *Christ* whom the doctrines are about. We believe and try to understand the doctrines about Christ in order to believe and understand the Christ they are about. Doctrine, in other words, illuminates the person of Christ and serves as the means by which we know, love, and therefore enter into communion with Christ.

There is a similar distinction between our *arguments* for the Catholic faith and the *faith itself.* Only the difference here is much greater than the difference between doctrines about Christ and Christ himself. For even though the doctrines about Christ remain formulations of truth in human language and are not Christ himself, they still accurately and truthfully, if not completely, express who and what Jesus Christ is. The Holy Spirit's guidance of the Church safeguards that—at least when the Church defines or proposes something to be definitively held.

But arguments for the faith are not *what* we believe as a matter of divine faith; nor are they generally vouchsafed by the Holy Spirit to lead us to believe. We may think our particular arguments for Catholicism true, but they remain purely human constructs without the benefit of the Holy Spirit's protection, which dogmas and even some other formulations of Catholic doctrine possess. The only safeguards they have are the truth itself, to the extent that they embody and lead to it, and our ability to assess the truth.

New and Improved

The quest for novel arguments poses another danger to the apologist's faith and to the faith of those influenced by such arguments. As more people have become—or aspire to become—professional Catholic apologists, the field itself has become more competitive. One way to stand out in the growing crowd of apologetics professionals is to concoct new arguments or clever explanations no one else has heard of, or at least that no one else has popularized.

New ideas and better explanations of "the faith once delivered to the saints" can indeed serve the cause of Christ. We should not be bashful about presenting new ideas; nor should we cling stubbornly to the old merely because it is old. Yet in the rush to devise a new angle on the faith, there is a real danger of reshaping

the faith to fit one's pet theories or ideas about it. At the very
least, there is a danger of overlooking weaknesses in a theory because it is innovative and provocative (not to mention because it
is *one's own*).

People too concerned with their place in the growing apologist
pantheon are not the only ones who are subject to confusing certain arguments for the faith with the faith itself. Many Catholics
who are not well schooled in the finer points of theology can be
misled by a popular theory or explanation and come to identify
it with the teaching of the Church herself. This is dangerous because the theory is not itself the teaching of the Church; and if
someone undermines or refutes the theory, people may think the
Catholic faith has been undermined or refuted. A related problem
arises when people are too swayed by the personality of a given
apologist and become apologetics groupies.

Jesus promised that the truth would set us free. He said nothing about your or my theory of the truth. If an apologist peddles
something as the truth that is actually false, it does not really free
anyone who buys into it. Of course some errors are, practically
speaking, innocuous. Besides, God can use anything, even my
mistakes, as stepping stones to bring me or others along the path
to truth. But the fact that God can salvage a botched situation
does not justify my botching things up in the first place. Nothing
justifies presenting novel ideas as if they were theological verities
or looking the other way when others pick up on my ideas as if
they were the gospel and spread them with the zeal that should
be reserved for God's word.

And there is another problem. What happens if, God forbid, a
popular apologist whose views are widely considered as if they
were *de fide* were himself to fall away or give public scandal? People who have too closely identified the *apologist's* faith with *the*
faith can be devastated. There is a danger of trying to believe on
someone else's intellectual, theological, or spiritual coattails.

Confusing our arguments, or someone else's, with the faith we
argue for is dangerous business, both for apologists and for those
influenced by them. On the one hand, it can lead us to think of

Catholicism, however subconsciously, as *our* idea or *our* intellectual achievement rather than as the truth God has graciously and mercifully shared with us. It can also, as we have seen, set us or others up for a big fall, should someone undermine or appear to undermine our arguments, or should a prominent defender of the faith, in whom we inordinately trust, falter.

In the final analysis, being a Catholic is not about having the best arsenal of clever arguments or about belonging to the Church with the best apologists formulating the best arguments. It is about humbly submitting to God, who is truth, and who can use Balaam's ass as effectively as he can the most eloquent and learned of apologists.

4

Contentiousness

We have considered the problems of reducing the faith to apologetics and to arguments in general (Deadly Sin Number Two) and to our own arguments in particular (Deadly Sin Number Three). Now we turn from arguments to argumentativeness.

The Fourth Deadly Sin of Catholic Apologetics is plain old argumentativeness, or, if you like, contentiousness. Some apologists are always looking for a fight. They go out of their way to reduce the faith to areas of disagreement with others or at least to put undue emphasis on disagreement. Thanks be to God that contentiousness between Catholics and non-Catholics today does not usually entail violence and bloodshed (Northern Ireland excepted). Nevertheless, contentious Catholics (and their non-Catholic counterparts), who "prowl around like lions seeking whom they may devour," can still do damage. Unfortunately, the damage is usually to the cause of Christ and his Church, although many contentious apologists do not or will not see it.

Differences

Obviously enough, contentiousness involves disagreement over differences, although for the well-practiced contentious person, it is not necessary to disagree with a man about something in order to argue with him. The trouble for the contentious apologist is that he does not know how to handle differences.

When it comes to religious differences, there are three options: we can exaggerate or accentuate them; we can ignore or minimize them; we can recognize them, give them their due, but keep them in their proper place in the scheme of things. The last is the best course, but taking it requires making distinctions, which some apologists, out of excessive zeal or prejudice, do not always do.

Some religious differences are largely if not purely terminological. The Eastern Orthodox talk about "the Divine Liturgy," while the Latin Catholics refer to "the Holy Sacrifice of the Mass." They are referring to the same thing. Other differences are matters of taste or emphasis. Baptists believe Jesus died on the cross for our sins but usually do not have crucifixes in their churches. For them, an empty cross speaks of Jesus' Resurrection. Catholics, who also believe Christ rose from the dead, put a corpus on the cross to proclaim that he died for our sins. There is no real difference of belief, only of emphasis.

Some religious differences entail real contradictions, on minor or major points. Muslims say Jesus was merely a prophet, inferior to Muhammad. In other words, they claim that Jesus is not God. Christians say he was—and is—God incarnate. Muslims and Christians cannot both be right about this, nor is this merely a difference of terminology or emphasis. These beliefs about Jesus cannot both be true: either Jesus is or is not God.

Thus, we can see that to treat all religious differences the same is a grave mistake. The apologist who does so risks unnecessarily alienating people from the Catholic faith by making more of a difference than is necessary or glossing over a difference that is crucial.

But even when he does not treat all differences the same, the contentious apologist can still fixate on them. Instead of understanding Catholicism in terms of the intrinsic structure of Catholic truth, he always places distinctive Catholic tenets at the very top of the "hierarchy of truths." He approaches the faith mainly in terms of what Catholics are against, instead of what we are for. In this way, the contentious Catholic apologist really becomes the anti-Protestant, anti-Orthodox, or anti-non-Christian apologist. As Christopher Derrick points out in his superb apologetical book *That Strange Divine Sea*, being Catholic means more than screaming, "The Protestants are wrong!" The Catholic faith has positive as well as negative aspects. But contentiousness tends to obscure that fact.

What We Are For

The core of Catholicism is an affirmation, not a denial. It is the Triune God and God's self-donating love and mercy toward us. It is communion with the Father, through the Son, in the Holy Spirit. That, ultimately, is what being a Catholic is all about. We Catholics should *defend* the Church, because we believe that the Catholic Church is *the* divinely established sacrament of communion with the Father, through the Son, in the Spirit. But we should not be *defensive*. We must earnestly contend for the faith (Jude 3) without being contentious (cf. Titus 3:9, 1 Pet. 3:15).

We Catholic apologists can fall into contentiousness if we take disagreements personally. That may sound strange if you think of being an apologist as a vocation or an avocation requiring professional or quasi-professional detachment and objectivity. But apologists are human, too, which means we are also susceptible to the intellectual and rhetorical blows of those who disagree with us.

Defending the faith is not supposed to be about us but about God and his truth. We should not defend Catholicism because *our* Church is being attacked; that is the attitude of the nationalist or sectarian. Still less should we be defensive because our personal beliefs are challenged—as if the Catholic faith were merely a matter of our private philosophy of life or personal theology. No, we should defend the Church because we love God and the Church belongs to him, and because we love our neighbors, and the Church—on the Catholic view—is the God-given means of bringing people into *full* communion with Christ, the only Savior. If we truly believe that, then charity compels us to share the truth of the Catholic faith with others.

In order to avoid the Deadly Sin of Contentiousness, we apologists should always keep before us the positive realities of the

Catholic faith: what we are *for* and why we are *for* it; or, better, *whom* we are for (i.e., the Triune God) and why. We should be more passionate about what we affirm than what we deny. Why? Because every denial the Church utters, every heretical proposition she condemns, every anathema she pronounces follows from an affirmation of something else. It is that "something else" we should never lose sight of.

Apologists should always remember that we oppose certain things because we stand for others. We reject Arianism, for example, because we affirm the full divinity of the Son. The Catholic apologist takes issue with Jehovah's Witnesses because they regard Jesus Christ as a mere creature rather than God incarnate. But it is the positive truth about Jesus (and genuine regard for the Jehovah's Witness, who is without that truth) that should motivate the Catholic apologist, not simply the chance to oppose an error or cut down an opponent.

Likewise the Catholic apologist denies *sola scriptura* because of a positive truth: the divine authority of Tradition and the Magisterium, as well as Scripture—even though, on the Catholic view, neither Tradition nor the Magisterium is divinely inspired as Scripture is. It is not because the Bible is somehow "un-Catholic" or defective. It is not even because traditional Protestants are wrong to uphold the divine word over any and every merely human word. On these points, traditional Protestantism is right, as Louis Bouyer brilliantly argued over half a century ago in *The Spirit and Forms of Protestantism*. No, Catholicism rejects *sola scriptura* because Christ continues to teach in and through his Church, both the Church of the Fathers (Tradition) and the Church today (the Magisterium), and what he teaches by these means is more than a mere human word. Out of fidelity to what we believe is the voice of Jesus himself and his word, the Catholic Church must reject the *sola scriptura* approach if it means denying authoritative, binding Tradition and the Magisterium.[1]

---

[1] I say "if it means denying authoritative, binding Tradition and the Magisterium" because not all forms of *sola scriptura* require a repudiation of Tradi-

When the Catholic apologist approaches *sola scriptura* in this way, he actually finds common ground with traditional Protestants, even though they accept *sola scriptura* and the Catholic apologist does not. The Catholic rejects the doctrine of *sola scriptura* because it is contrary to God's word. To embrace it would, on the Catholic view, amount to subordinating God's word (what God has revealed about his truth and how it is presented in the Church) to what the Catholic regards as a human idea. This is also exactly why the traditional Protestant affirms *sola scriptura* and rejects Tradition and the Magisterium: he thinks that they elevate a merely human word over the divine word. Thus, the opposite positions Catholics and Protestants take on Scripture, Tradition, and Magisterium are based on the same underlying principle, the supremacy of the divine word over the merely human word. The disagreement is over exactly how God intends that supremacy to be upheld.

There are ways, then, to summarize disagreements between Catholics and non-Catholics that allow us, despite our real differences, to see the common ground between us. The work of finding this common ground is sometimes called "ecumenical apologetics," a subject we will consider in more detail in chapter 10, in which a related issue, the nature of true dialogue, is discussed. The point here is that the contentious apologist goes out of his way to state things in the most polemical manner, thus pushing non-Catholics further from the Catholic faith. Rather than starting with what we have in common and seeing how far we can walk down the theological road together, a contentious apolo-

---

tion and the Magisterium. Some Catholic theologians have argued that it is possible for a Catholic to hold that all divine revelation can be found in the Bible, in one form or another. That would mean that the Bible is "materially sufficient" as a source of Christian belief and practice. At the same time, Catholics are obliged to accept the authority of Tradition and the Magisterium. That precludes the Bible from being "formally sufficient." Even if all divine revelation is contained in the Bible in some manner or other, Tradition and the Magisterium are still necessary to expound it accurately and authoritatively for the community of the Church.

gist immediately zeroes in on what separates Catholics and non-Catholics. He formulates the Catholic position in the most anti-non-Catholic way he can think of. He may do this in an openly aggressive way or with a smile upon his face, but in either case he creates a problem.

A Recent Example

The reaction of some apologists to the recent *Lutheran-Catholic Joint Declaration on Justification* illustrates the point about contentiousness. The document has been highly praised in many Catholic circles, yet some highly reputable theologians have expressed their concerns about certain aspects of the statement. In a widely noted article in *First Things* (December 1999), Jesuit theologian Avery Dulles—certainly no contentious apologist—raised important questions about how to reconcile some elements of the *Joint Declaration* with the Council of Trent. According to Dulles, the declaration's rendition of Catholic teaching on merit "seems to fall short of what Catholics believe and what Trent teaches under anathema." Whether Dulles is right about that or about other points of concern, the document is obviously not above criticism, so the mere fact that an apologist questions it should not be taken as implying he is being contentious.

At the same time, some apologists have downplayed or ignored the declaration because, despite John Paul II's having called the document "a blessing," they do not like agreeing with something that refers to Lutherans, or Protestants in general, as anything less than full-blown heretics. For the contentious apologists, Protestants are people to argue with and to refute, not partners with whom to enter into ecumenical agreements. Such apologists will accept nothing short of the Lutherans saying, "We were wrong about justification, and the Catholic Church is completely right."

This attitude neglects a crucial fact: a sizable number of Lutherans have agreed to the proposition that the Catholic Church's view of justification is not heretical. That is a *major* ecumenical breakthrough, a tremendous step in the right direction—and one accomplished without substantive compromise of Catholic doctrine. Of course, Catholics would, ideally, like to see things progress much further—as would the Lutheran participants, though obviously in a different direction. But it is a start. That we got less than the ideal does not mean we have achieved little or nothing.

Other Problems

Contentious apologetics can also lead to unnecessary gibes at non-Catholics. One apologist, addressing the topic of the Church and slavery, went out of his way to take potshots at Protestants. Protestant countries, he claimed, pushed slavery on the world, while the Catholic Church condemned it. Catholic slave traders or slave owners were identified as "Spaniards" or "Portuguese" rather than Catholics; slave traders or slave owners from the United States or England were described as coming from "Protestant countries."

The popes certainly condemned chattel slavery since its revival in the fifteenth century, yet many Catholics, including some Catholic bishops in the American South, approved of it or at least tried to undercut the force of papal condemnations. The papacy was a foe of chattel slavery, but so were many English and American Protestants. Evangelical Protestants, not Catholics, dominated abolitionism. It is unfair, then, to suggest that there was something peculiarly Protestant about chattel slavery or to depict Catholics as solidly opposed to it and Protestants as peddling it. It was, after all, *Catholic* traders, not Protestants, who reintroduced slavery into Europe in the first place.

I do not mention these things to undercut Catholic claims or to suggest that the return of slavery was a natural outgrowth of Catholicism. Indeed, the Catholic Church in the Middle Ages all but eliminated slavery. The Age of Exploration saw its return because men were insufficiently Catholic—insufficiently aware of our common redemption in Christ—not because they were *too* Catholic. My point is that contentiousness can lead to misstatements and dishonesty in favor of Catholicism at the truth's expense. Insecure Catholics may feel better about themselves because of it, but it will hardly make Catholicism more plausible to the informed non-Catholic.

Another problem with contentiousness is that it often leads Catholic apologists to delight in "knocking the other guy down." The martial spirit takes over, and soon an apologist argues for the sheer joy of trouncing his opponents or showing off his superior knowledge or debating skills. Unfortunately, some Catholic apologists come across as gloating when they have refuted—or think they have refuted—their non-Catholic antagonists. One apologist I know claims Protestants must be either stupid or liars to hold their views. His polemical style reminds me of one of Sheed's anti-Catholic hecklers who shouted, "Either you're paid to say these things or you're mentally deficient. And I can't imagine anybody paying you."

You may ask, "What *do* you do when your opponent utters nonsense against Christ or the Church?" It is easier to say what you should not do. The general rule the Catholic Evidence Guild followed was never to make a joke at the expense of someone who offers a question or comment, even a hostile or foolish one. The best advice in that regard I personally ever received came from Karl Keating, who said, "Let your opponent's foolishness speak for itself. Your job is to present the truth as winsomely as possible." After all, what do you really accomplish in a battle of wits with a fool? If you belittle or make jokes about him, it probably will reflect badly on you and your message.

People such as Frank Sheed, with decades of street corner experience, claim that the rare exceptions to the rule do not justify changing the general policy—though Sheed once told of such an exception worth mentioning. A rather unattractive, obnoxious woman heckling a guild speaker shouted this allegation: "Your priests send young men from the confessional to make love to me!" To which the platform speaker replied, "I did not realize they were giving out such strict penances these days." The speaker was not reprimanded.

Sheed himself occasionally gave in to the urge to hurl a jocular comeback. An atheist heckler had been going on and on about how he could make a better world than God made. After a bit, Sheed shot back, "Would you mind making a rabbit for us, just to establish confidence?" This is a bit like the story of what God said to the scientist who claimed he could replicate man, given the same circumstances God used. The scientist bent over to pick up a handful of dirt, to which God said, "Get your own dirt!"

Rare exceptions, then, do not invalidate the general rule about not putting down one's opponent. When Catholic apologists become contentious, their good sense sometimes disappears and, too often with it, any consideration the non-Catholic might have given to the faith. Here the apologist would do well to remember 1 Peter 3:15 *and* 16. "Always be prepared to make a defense to anyone who calls you to account for the hope that is in you," Peter writes, adding, perhaps with the contentious apologist in mind, "yet do it with gentleness and reverence; and keep your conscience clear, so that, when you are abused, those who revile your good behavior in Christ may be put to shame."

5

Friendly Fire

Not distinguishing enemies from allies is the Fifth Deadly Sin of Catholic Apologetics. We are in the middle of a culture war in the West. Many people whose theology we Catholics cannot wholly subscribe to are, nevertheless, on our side in the culture war. To use the late Evangelical thinker Francis Schaeffer's term, they are "cobelligerents." We must be able to distinguish allies from true enemies on an issue.

In the grand scheme of things, it is not Catholics vs. Protestants so much as believers vs. unbelievers; absolutists vs. relativists. It is truth vs. error, with the old serpent, the Father of Lies, using others to front for him. Consequently, we risk unintentionally shooting an ally (or ourselves in the foot) by always aiming our apologetical firepower so close to home—at those nearest us theologically—or, at the other extreme, by shooting at anything that moves on the non-Catholic theological landscape.

Consider some of those who are theologically closest to us. Evangelicals, for example, accept more or less the same Bible as Catholics. They believe in the same Triune God, the incarnation, death, and resurrection of Christ, the reality of heaven and hell, the divine founding of the Church, and so on. Sharing so much in common with Evangelicals, Catholic apologists can assume a great deal from the outset, which makes engaging in apologetical discussion relatively easy. Not surprisingly, then, most of contemporary Catholic apologetics centers on the Catholic-Evangelical/Fundamentalist debate. Most apologetics books and audiotapes reflect that discussion. Most apologetics magazines feature articles on the subject.

It is easier to talk with Evangelicals or Fundamentalists, but is that where our apologetical focus should be? If you were the lone Catholic apologist in a room full of religiously diverse people interested in discussing religion, would you zero in on the Evangelical or Fundamentalist Christians and start arguing about the papacy, say, or justification by faith alone? Many apologists would not, but more than a few I know would. Meanwhile, the non-Christians would be ignored. More likely than not, they would also be scandalized by Christians bickering among themselves. The moral: as Catholic apologists, we must guard against a preoccupation with Evangelicalism and Fundamentalism that leads us to ignore the wider mission of talking with non-Christians.

As I say, the man who believes in God but holds no definite creed is in many ways much harder to talk to than the Baptist, who believes in God and in Jesus Christ as the Son of God. But those without set religious beliefs or a specific creed are by far the larger group today and certainly in more need of evangelization than most Baptists, who, from the Catholic perspective, are already halfway home. This is not to say that Catholic apologists should not engage Evangelicals or Fundamentalists, only that we must discern the proper time and place for it. We should not spend all our time and energy arguing with those who know Christ while neglecting those who do not.

When the blasphemous movie *The Last Temptation of Christ* was released back in the 1980s, a few Catholic friends and I protested it at a local theater. Some ex-Catholic Fundamentalists also showed up. To everyone's surprise, so did an Orthodox Jew. Interestingly, he was there to denounce the film as mocking a Jewish religious figure, Jesus of Nazareth, even though the man did not think Jesus was the Messiah or the Son of God. The whole thing looked like an odd ecumenical and interreligious shindig right out on the sidewalk in front of the theater, until the ex-Catholics began "witnessing" to the Catholics.

You probably know the tune: Catholics are not Christians because they trust in good works rather than Christ as Savior, the pope is Antichrist, the Catholic Church is the Whore of Babylon, and so on. Unfortunately, we Catholics let ourselves get sucked into a debate, much to the disservice of our Christian witness to the unbelievers around us. For a moment I thought of postponing this admittedly important discussion to another time or taking it to another place, but we did not. Instead, we provided a spectacle of Christians, ostensibly united to defend Jesus Christ, bickering among ourselves before the unbelieving world. I do not know what those in the ticket line thought about it, but the Jewish man was stunned. "Why waste so much time arguing with each other?" he chided. "Why not defend the man you believe to be the Messiah? You can argue over these other things somewhere else!"

A Caveat

We must be careful here. Some Catholics do not want Catholics to try to persuade Protestants to become Catholics. "They are already Christians. Why bother with them?" The obvious answer is that Christ wants his followers to have *all* he has revealed (Matt. 28:20), *all* the means of grace he has made available, and *all* the guidance his shepherds can provide. If a Catholic believes those things exist fully only in the Catholic Church, it follows that, out of fidelity to Christ, he should try to share them with his Protestant brethren. If he does not, one may question the extent to which he really believes the Catholic Church to be the fullness of Christianity.

Let me be clear. I am not arguing that Catholics and Protestants should *never* discuss or debate differences—we should. Indeed, under certain circumstances, we must. But doing so is a question of time, place, approach, and priority. When the issue is whether Christ founded the Catholic Church, Catholics and Protestants— out of their mutual loyalty to Jesus—must discuss their differences. And when anti-Catholic Fundamentalists proselytize Catholics or when conservative Evangelicals challenge Catholic tenets, Catholic apologists have a right and a duty to respond with charity, which includes offering the best arguments for the faith that we can muster. Yet when issues of concern to all Christians arise or when we come together to express our common Christian commitment, we must (at least temporarily) set our differences aside and work together. We must, in other words, have the spiritual wherewithal to discern when to do what with whom.

Ecumenism and the Catholic Apologist

Some apologists have trouble here because when it comes to dialogue with non-Catholic Christians, they have only half of the equation. These apologists rightly want to present Catholic truth as the fullness of the Christian faith, but they do not necessarily know how to discuss their faith with non-Catholic Christians without entering into full-blown apologetical arguments. They may be great when it comes to arguments, but they seem to be lost when it comes to ecumenism. Among other things, ecumenism means stressing (and valuing) what we Christians have in common, as well as discussing our differences. Both elements are needed if we are to attain the full unity Christ wills for his followers. And both elements have a role to play in the Church's mission.

Part of the problem, I suspect, is that some apologists either do not completely understand or do not fully embrace the Church's teaching on ecumenism. I say that knowing full well that some apologists will dismiss the charge as warmed-over theological liberalism. After all, that is what they usually hear from theological dissenters who do not really believe that Christ founded the Catholic Church in any meaningful sense of the phrase. Even so, I believe there is some truth to the charge, as even a cursory comparison of the Church's teaching with some apologists' practices reveals.

According to Vatican II's Decree on Ecumenism, *Unitatis Red-*

integratio, Catholics must make "every effort to eliminate words, judgments, and actions which do not correspond to the condition of separated brethren with truth and fairness and so make mutual relations between them more difficult" (4). Yet how often do we hear Catholic apologists mischaracterize Protestant theology or fail to distinguish among the various Protestant positions on certain subjects? Often, the underlying attitude is this: since the Catholic Church is ultimately right and Protestantism of whatever stripe is ultimately wrong, what does it matter if the Catholic apologist confuses Reformed doctrine with Methodism, or Baptist beliefs with Presbyterianism? Who can keep straight all the varieties of Protestantism, anyway? But difficult or not, correctly representing non-Catholic beliefs is part of the Church's ecumenical teaching. The topic of accuracy in depicting non-Catholic views is important enough to return to it in chapter 6.

But there is more. Catholic ecumenism should affect how Catholics talk about their faith *with one another*. According to the Vatican's *Directory for the Application of the Principles and Norms of Ecumenism* (61), catechesis should help form a genuinely ecumenical attitude in Catholics by, among other means, expounding "clearly, with charity and with due firmness, the whole doctrine of the Catholic Church respecting in a particular way the order of the hierarchy of truths and avoiding expressions and ways of presenting doctrine which would be an obstacle to dialogue."

There are at least two things to note there. First, we must respect "the hierarchy of truths." The truths of the faith vary in their respective relations to the central and foundational mystery of the faith, the Holy Trinity (CCC 90, 234). The "hierarchy of truths" does not mean—as it has often been taken to mean—that some truths of the faith are dispensable or less true than others. It does mean that more central truths are, well, more central. Some dogmas rest upon others, the latter helping us understand the former (*Mysterium Ecclesiae,* "The Church's Gift of Infallibility Not to be Diminished").

What does this mean for ecumenism? Among other things, it means that when comparing Catholic and non-Catholic beliefs, we should note where a given doctrine stands in that "hierarchy." Doing that helps Catholics and non-Catholics understand better how close or far apart they are and how much their differences matter. It can also help Catholics and non-Catholics overcome those differences or at least move closer together. For example, an Evangelical Protestant will probably be less inclined to denounce, say, the doctrine of Mary's Immaculate Conception if he knows that Catholics predicate things of Mary because of her relation to Christ and the Church. In the hierarchy of truths, Catholic teaching about Mary is subordinate to and dependent upon the truth about Christ; it does not stand on its own.

In addition to respecting the hierarchy of truths, Catholic apologists must avoid expressions and ways of presenting doctrine that impede dialogue. Vatican II states that "the manner and order in which Catholic belief is expressed should in no way become an obstacle to dialogue with our brethren" (*Unitatis Redintegratio* 11). While warning against "a false irenicism that harms the purity of Catholic doctrine and obscures its genuine and certain meaning," the council nevertheless insists that "Catholic belief must be explained more profoundly and precisely, in such a way and in such terms that our separated brethren can also really understand it."

Commenting on the council's teaching, John Paul II says, "Certainly it is possible to profess one's faith and to explain its teaching in a way that is correct, fair, and understandable, and which at the same time takes into account both the way of thinking and the actual historical experiences of the other party" (*Ut Unum Sint* 36).

We can add a third point: there is a distinction between the deposit of faith and how it is expressed. This is an often-repeated teaching in magisterial documents on ecumenism (UR 6). Like the notion of the hierarchy of truths, it has sometimes been distorted by dissenters and others, so we should take care to get it straight. It does not mean formulations of the faith are infinitely malleable, or that given enough time and hard work, we can always find a formula to reconcile conflicting views. It means that in some cases it may be possible to express the same truth, without compromise, in another way—a way perhaps more acceptable to non-Catholics. This, it appears, is what happened in the 1994 *Common Christological Declaration between the Catholic Church and the Assyrian Church of the East* and in *The Joint Declaration on Justification between the Catholic Church and the Lutheran World Federation.* Even where reformulation of a doctrine does not lead to complete communion on a particular point, it can still diminish the range of disagreement. And *that* can open the way to full communion down the road.

As Catholic apologists, then, we should keep the Church's ecumenical teaching in mind in discerning when, how, and with whom to engage in apologetical argument. We should recall what we have in common with non-Catholics, as well as where we differ with them. We should not mischaracterize non-Catholic beliefs or introduce *unnecessary* obstacles to dialogue by the way we formulate Catholic beliefs.

Cutting Them Some Slack

I have leveled some strong criticisms at some Catholic apologists for not following Vatican II's teaching on ecumenism. Let me balance things with the observation that, in most cases, these apologists do not mean to reject the council; they are reacting to a widespread misunderstanding and distortion of Vatican II, the idea that other Christians ought not to be encouraged to become Catholics. Many converts, especially former Protestant ministers, recount how, when they first approached a priest about becoming Catholic, they were greeted with, "Why do you want to do that? You can do so much more good for Christian unity staying where you are." In one case I know of, the would-be convert was not only told to stay put, but the priest actually tried vigorously to argue against some key Catholic beliefs the prospective convert had already come to accept!

Converts are not the only ones put off by such seeming indifference to the truth-claims of the Catholic Church. Many cradle Catholics are tired of their loved ones and friends leaving the Catholic Church, at least in part because no one seems able to defend the Church or refute the attacks upon her. Catholic apologists give their fellow Catholics confidence, not to mention some desperately sought answers to the seemingly irrefutable objections posed by anti-Catholic proselytizers. That leads many an ordinary Catholic-in-the-pew to exclaim, "It is about time someone did something," and some Catholic apologists to conclude that ecumenical discussion is a losing proposition.

Besides, the ones most aggressively attacking the Church and snatching Catholics away from her seem the least willing to engage in ecumenical discussion. Many of them regard Catholicism as a satanic plot to institute a one-world religious system, the Whore of Babylon mentioned in the book of Revelation. The pope, on this view, is the Antichrist or at least a precursor to the Antichrist. Any attempt at genuine ecumenical dialogue is rebuffed as a demonically inspired effort to distort the gospel.

Obviously, it is difficult for Catholics to discuss Christianity with people who think that way, and very easy for us to slip into a mode of contentiousness. But we must still resist the temptation. Not all non-Catholic Christians hold such views. Those who do hold them need our charity, patience, and understanding, as well as good apologetical arguments.

Instructing the Ignorant

Another source of confusion about allies and enemies is a misunderstanding of the Church's teaching on invincible ignorance and non-Catholics. Some apologists seem to think that invincible ignorance means sheer ignorance that cannot be overcome with a reasonable effort. Thus, they think that once Catholicism has been explained to the intelligent Protestant, for instance, he can no longer be invincibly ignorant of it. If he remains a Protestant, he cannot be saved. His remaining a Protestant in such a situation only proves to some apologists that he is not a good man. He is, they think, an enemy, not an ally, of truth.

We should be clear: those who hold this view do not deny that non-Catholics can be saved. They simply think that reasonable non-Catholics who have heard the case for the Catholic Church can no longer be invincibly ignorant. If such a non-Catholic fails to convert, it must be because he is, in his heart of hearts, stubbornly opposing the truth and, therefore, stubbornly opposing God himself. Under those circumstances, it is not possible for a man to be saved, since being saved essentially entails turning to God. One who opposes God cannot at the same time turn to him.

The trouble with this scenario is that it does not accurately represent Catholic teaching about ignorance and culpability. Invincible ignorance does not mean one is merely ignorant, through no fault of his own, of *what* the Catholic Church teaches; it means one is ignorant of its *truth*—of the *fact* that it is true—through no fault of his own. Thus, merely presenting Catholic teaching to, say, an intelligent Protestant does not mean he can no longer be invincibly ignorant. For after all is said and done, after the Catholic apologist has framed the best arguments he can and after the Protestant has investigated Catholicism honestly and to the best of his ability, the Protestant may still (erroneously and mysteriously, perhaps) think that Catholicism is false or less than completely true. If the Protestant were to become a Catholic under those circumstances, he would be embracing what he thinks is untrue. And *that* would amount to sin, not salvation for him.

Jews and Muslims

The problem of mistaking allies for enemies is not limited to our approach to other Christians. We see something similar with other religious believers, although it is less obvious to us because so few Catholic apologists ever engage non-Christians. Take, for example, Jewish believers. It is a grave error to think Christians should never present Jesus as the Messiah to Jewish people, as if

Christianity were an exclusively Gentile affair and Christ did not include the Jewish people in his command to make disciples of *all* nations (Matt. 28:19). That mistaken notion, widely circulated as the teaching of Vatican II, is bolstered by the fear many Catholics have of being labeled anti-Semitic. For some people, any effort to convince a Jewish person that Jesus is the Messiah, no matter how politely undertaken or respectfully carried out, is plain old anti-Semitism and tantamount to a hate crime.

We can understand the overreaction, in the context of that great twentieth-century blackness called the Holocaust. We can also understand how it has been fed by centuries of Christian anti-Semitism and persecution of Jews. Even so, Christians are obliged to tell Jewish people, as they are obliged to tell every people, about Jesus Christ, the Savior of the world. Yet when we do, we must not dismiss God's covenant with Abraham, Isaac, and Jacob as utterly void. Nor should we turn every encounter between Christians and Jews into a proselytizing session (as some Fundamentalist Protestants do) or overlook the vast heritage we share with traditional Judaism, especially regarding morality. Some of traditional Christianity's staunchest allies are Orthodox Jews.

Muslims, too, can be cobelligerents in the culture war. People have become aware that there are many Muslims in America. In fact, there are more Muslims than there are Episcopalians. Thus, we can no longer ignore Muslims, either as people to engage in discussion regarding the gospel or as allies against secularism.

Regarding the first of those last two points, Catholic apologetics' preoccupation with Protestantism has hampered the development of an effective apologetic vis-à-vis Islam. Until recently, that has not been much of a problem. With rare exception, you have to go back to fifteenth-century Spain to find serious and sustained discussions between Catholic and Muslim apologists. But as Islam continues to spread throughout America, Europe, and elsewhere, Catholics will have to think about how to engage it. And it will not do to dig through the same bag of apologetics tricks we use with traditional Protestants. Muslims cannot be refuted by arguments against *sola scriptura* or *sola fide*, or by showing that Peter is the rock in Matthew 16:18.

In some ways, we must approach Islam as we approach Judaism, as a religion focused on God and his Covenant. But unlike Judaism, Islam has some definite views about Jesus and his place in the history of God's dealing with man. Muslims—they do not like being called Mohammedans, since they do not worship Muhammad as Christians worship Christ—believe they are truer to the religion of Jesus than we Christians. Muslims have an elaborate theological system in which Jesus plays an important, though subordinate, role to that of Muhammad. Christian apologists have to show how their view of Jesus fits the facts far better than Islam's view, without undermining the truths Muslims already possess. And all this takes time—time to get to know what Muslims really believe (and Catholics should be warned against taking at face value certain extreme Fundamentalist Protestant interpretations of Islam), time to show Muslims how many of their ideas about Christ and Christians are mistaken.

On many moral and social issues, Muslims stand with the Catholic Church. The Vatican found that out several years ago at the United Nations' International Conference on Population and Development (1994) in Cairo, Egypt. When the purveyors of abortion and contraception tried to impose their antifamily agenda on the Third World, Islamic nations stood by Vatican efforts to defend human life, the family, and the dignity of the human person. Like traditional Protestants and Jews, therefore, Muslims can be allies in the social and political arenas.

We can extend this approach to other religions as well—to non-Western belief systems, for example. Fewer points of contact exist there, and the areas of disagreement are larger. Nevertheless, we can find some measure of agreement without ignoring differences or minimizing the gospel message.

The Bottom Line

Peter Kreeft has called for an ecumenical front of believers (of all sorts) against unbelief and secularism. By that, Kreeft does not mean Catholics should become religious indifferentists, holding one religion is as good as another. Nor does he suggest we should never argue with those who disagree. He does so himself in his various books of apologetics. He means we should unite as far as we can, without compromising our commitment to the truth. Unfortunately, some Catholic apologists have not heeded Kreeft's ecumenical call to arms. By indiscriminately machine-gunning everyone in sight, including would-be allies, some overly aggressive apologists unwittingly weaken our side of the war effort. In this spiritual battle, we cannot afford casualties lost to friendly fire.

6

Trying to "Win"

In the game King of the Hill, children struggle to capture and hold the top of a hill, using almost any tactic they can get away with. The objective is to win, not to help others to the top. The Sixth Deadly Sin of Catholic Apologetics involves trying to "win the argument"—to be King of the Apologetical Hill—even at the expense of bringing people to truth. In a sense, this is an obvious temptation for apologists, given that apologetics, like lawyering, is about arguments. But unlike some lawyers, apologists are not allowed to fashion their arguments in order to attain a certain verdict. The apologist's goal has to be "the truth, the whole truth, and nothing but the truth," whatever a lawyer's may be.

Vince Lombardi, a Catholic, is credited with the line, "Winning isn't everything; it's the only thing." People have argued over what he meant. But however Lombardi's maxim may apply to football, it certainly does not work with apologetics. Frank Sheed, the Vince Lombardi of Catholic apologetics if ever there was one, warned Catholic Evidence Guild speakers about going for "victory." How tempting to use apologetics to trounce the other guy, especially if he is unskilled in debate or unfamiliar with the theological terrain. The trouble, said Sheed, is that when you set out to win in this way, you create problems. You tend to soft-pedal the weaknesses of your argument, neglect the strength of the other fellow's, and, most important, set up barriers for the Holy Spirit in that person's heart (not to mention your own).

Few of us enjoy being bested in argument. Sometimes the experience can push a person further from the truth. As Archbishop Fulton Sheen used to say, "Win an argument, lose a soul." In fact, it is much better to let someone discover the truth for himself than to try to browbeat him into submission to your case for the truth.

An overweening desire to win the argument can lead apologists into other mistakes, such as using *any* apologetical stick to beat an opponent. The man out to win at all costs never met an argument against a non-Catholic position he did not like. He may even misrepresent facts in favor of the Catholic Church or against non-Catholics. Winning is the most important thing to him, and if the facts make it harder to win, then the facts be damned.

A Case in Point

The Inquisition is an example of a topic where facts sometimes suffer at the hands of certain Catholic apologists. Some Catholic apologists do not tell the whole Inquisition story. They distort the historical record because the Church does not come out so clearly on the side of the angels as these apologists would like when the facts of the Inquisition are looked at straight on. And when the Church does not come out looking its best, it is harder for the Catholic apologist to win the argument with the non-Catholic.

The standard anti-Catholic charge claims that the Inquisition slaughtered millions of people. The tally is ninety-five million, according to the Fundamentalist book *The Mystery of Babylon Revealed*, or twenty million, as televangelist Jimmy Swaggart has claimed. There is nothing wrong with setting the record straight about such nonsense, of course, provided you do not get lost in the "wilderness of comparative atrocity statistics," as Ronald Knox put it. Indeed, all things being equal, the Catholic apologist must refute such an outlandish charge.

Taking the best scholarly estimates of the number of deaths resulting from the Inquisition in its various forms and then multiplying by ten, you still arrive at a figure less than one-half of one percent of that claimed in *The Mystery of Babylon Revealed* and about two percent of Swaggart's. To be sure, that is still too many deaths, but it is not the wholesale slaughter on the order of magnitude anti-Catholics often claim the Inquisition to have been.

Some Catholic apologists go to the other extreme, though, and make the Inquisition out to have been a really good thing that has gotten a bum rap. But was it good that the Church approved of torture to compel people to recant heresy or what was taken to be heresy? It is not simply that the Inquisition was sometimes abused, as some apologists claim; the Inquisition's policy of using torture was itself an abuse, an abuse of human beings and of the authority of the Church. Yes, by all means let us qualify the point lest the Church's enemies pounce on it. Judicial practice of the time, the general outlook toward heresy, and the desperate circumstances surrounding the establishment of the Inquisition, such as the Albigensian threat, help us understand how popes, bishops, and even great and wise saints such as Thomas Aquinas and Dominic could mistakenly accept torture. Yes, by comparison with the secular courts of the day, the Inquisition looks pretty good. All of that said, it remains true that forcing people to recant on pain of torture is wrong—a *terrible* thing, not a basically good thing misused.

In defense of the Church, some apologists raise perfectly valid points about the Inquisition. But others overreach. Consider, for example, the argument that torture was common in the legal system of the day, in part the result of the medieval recovery of Roman law, which sometimes also employed torture to achieve its objectives. That helps us understand *how* the Church could go from forbidding torture under the ninth-century Pope Nicholas I, who said it was "against all laws, human and divine," to using torture under the thirteenth-century Pope Innocent IV. But that does not excuse anything; it only helps us understand and explain it.

Another common response is, "They did it, too." Protestants, some Catholic apologists are quick to point out, also tortured or killed people with whom they disagreed. True enough—at least in some cases—and even a helpful point if it gets an anti-Catholic to understand the mindset of the age and how even people he regards as otherwise respectable men could resort to violence in the name of Christ. Yet the honest skeptic may very well say, "A pox on both your houses!"

Some Protestants may sidestep the issue of other Protestants using violence to further their ends. Protestants, standing as they do on the Bible alone, do not think they have to defend what other Protestants have done or explain how a Protestant's actions can be so at odds with genuine Christian discipleship. After all, they will say, they stand under the authority of the Bible, not what other professed Protestants do or fail to do. If other Protestants have sinned, what has that to do with anything?

We Catholics do not have it so easy. We *do* have something to explain: how the infallible, indefectible, and holy Church of Christ can have leaders who not only sin but put in place policies and procedures diametrically opposed to the gospel, yet without ceasing to belong to Christ's Church or without the Church ceasing to be Christ's Church. And it is not just a question of *leaders*, but even some canonized *saints*. Yes, we *can* explain it, logically and even convincingly, but it takes some effort and a disposition on the part of our hearers to listen to the explanation and make subtle distinctions. Even so, we must be willing to address the dark, unpleasant facts about the Inquisition head-on, not spin them in our favor, ignore them or deny the undeniable.

Then there is the argument based on the social upheaval caused by dangerous heresies such as Catharism. The argument has much to commend it. When civil society is threatened, as medieval society was, by the sort of fanaticism found in Catharism, it often reacts (or overreacts) in a violent fashion to restore stability and to protect the common good. This argument, too, helps us understand the social pressures and influences that led many saints and sinners alike to support what we now understand to be inhumane, repressive measures. Yet the Church still authorized the police power of the state—Catholic states—to compel people to confess the faith under threat of torture or capital punishment (burning at the stake). That aspect of the Inquisition was grievously wrong, and the Church's credibility has suffered immensely for it.

The Inquisition Done Right

Perhaps the best example in contemporary apologetics of how to treat the Inquisition correctly is Karl Keating's chapter on it in *Catholicism and Fundamentalism*. Keating refutes anti-Catholic misconceptions about the Inquisition without succumbing to the temptation to whitewash it as a good thing or even a good thing gone amiss. Regarding the cruel procedures of the Inquisition, Keating concludes, "One should not seek to justify them, but to explain them and, most importantly, to explain how they could have been associated with a divinely established Church and how, from their existence, it is not proper to conclude that the Church of Rome is not the Church of Christ. This is where any discussion should focus."

The bottom line: the apologist must explain the evils of the Inquisition, not defend them, not explain them away. He must, as Keating argues, get at what the anti-Catholic thinks the Inquisition proves. Certain members of the Catholic Church have done wicked things? Guilty. The Church can err, in the prudential order? Guilty again. Catholics, like others who believe something strongly, can allow their zeal to mislead them into acting contrary to their own principles, properly understood? That is certainly true. But it does not prove what the anti-Catholic thinks it proves —that the Catholic Church is not the Church of Christ or that Catholicism is uniquely wicked in the history of religion. *That is* the point the Catholic apologist must drive home.

We can understand why apologists might be tempted to "style" the facts when it comes to the Inquisition. The facts are bad enough, and they are often distorted in order to attack the Catholic Church *as such* rather than the individuals responsible for the Inquisition. When John Paul II decided to ask forgiveness for the evils of the Inquisition, a number of cardinals reacted against the idea. Asking for forgiveness would be used against the Church, they argued. John Paul, undeterred, urged caution when dealing with the subject, precisely because it is so easy to jump to wrong conclusions and all too easy to judge other people glibly, with twenty-twenty moral hindsight.[1]

Nevertheless, in his apostolic letter in preparation for the Jubilee Year of 2000, *Tertio Millennio Adveniente*, the Holy Father declared, "Another painful chapter of history to which the sons and daughters of the Church must return with a spirit of repentance is that of the acquiescence given, especially in certain centuries, to intolerance and even the use of violence in the service of truth." He went on to say that "the consideration of mitigating factors does not exonerate the Church from the obligation to express profound regret for the weaknesses of so many of her sons and daughters who sullied her face, preventing her from fully mirroring the image of her crucified Lord, the supreme witness of patient love and of humble meekness." He also pointed to the need for Christians to draw lessons from this for the future, quoting Vatican II's *Declaration on Religious Freedom*, "The truth cannot impose itself except by virtue of its own truth, as it wins over the mind with both gentleness and power" (35).

I have picked the Inquisition as an illustration, but we could have chosen other topics as well. My point is, when you set out to win the argument, you may wind up defeating truth in the process. Besides, what happens when your apologetical sparring partner does a little research and discovers things are not as simple or pleasant as you have made out? What happens to your credibility with him in other areas? No one is well served by a less than wholly honest argument, and when you set out to win at all costs, it is usually very hard to make wholly honest arguments.

Accuracy

Honesty is one thing; accuracy, another. It is possible to be honest but inaccurate, so warnings about the need for honesty do

---

[1] On this point, see Pope John Paul II's October 31, 1998 Address to the International Symposium on the Inquisition held at the Vatican.

not solve the whole problem. For the unreflective apologist—yes, there are such people—the drive to win the argument can lead to serious inaccuracies, even when the apologist would never dream of being dishonest.

My favorite example here concerns certain Catholic apologists and the Eucharist. Many Catholic apologists are above reproach in their handling of the subject, making all the proper distinctions that others neglect. My comments, then, are not an indictment of Catholic apologists in general. Still, I cannot number how many times I have heard overeager Catholic apologists refer to "the Protestant position on the Eucharist." That is a mistake on at least two counts: first, because there are *many* Protestant positions on the Eucharist, not one; second, because the particular position intended—the symbolic interpretation—cannot really be dubbed "Protestant," even though some Protestants hold it. It was advocated long before there were any Protestants. Berengarius of Tours held a symbolical view of the Eucharist, as far as we can determine, and he certainly was no Protestant.

But back to the first point. Some popular apologetical presentations contrast the Catholic view of the Eucharist with "the Protestant view." On the Catholic view, Jesus Christ is really, truly, and substantially present under the appearances of bread and wine. The so-called Protestant view, so the argument goes, is that he is not there at all. The Catholic view is the doctrine of the Real Presence, the Protestant, the "Real Absence." All fine and good, except that Orthodox Christians also share the Catholic view, and quite a number of bona fide Protestants believe in the Real Presence.

We can set aside the fact that Catholics and Orthodox both affirm the Real Presence, more or less in the same sense. The Catholic can argue that this is a matter of Catholic doctrine that the Orthodox happen to share. Besides, he may add, Orthodoxy is such a relatively minor blip on the apologist's screen that he should, for immediate purposes, bracket it out of the discussion. That second point I am not so sure of. Orthodoxy is growing in some areas, and why not stress that the vast majority of Christians, Orthodox as well as Catholics, agree about the Real Presence? That certainly appears to be the stronger apologetical tack.

The real issue for me, though, is leaving out Protestants who affirm some version of the Real Presence. Lutherans, Anglicans, and some Reformed churches do not reduce the Eucharist to a mere symbol. Whether their belief is consubstantiation or virtualism or some variation of the same, those Protestants do not deny the Real Presence *as such*. Catholic apologists should take issue with what we believe are incomplete, dubious, or false renditions of the Real Presence, in whatever form. But we should not mischaracterize those positions as symbolic or neglect them because we like the convenience of railing against a monolithic "Protestant view." That is just plain wrong.

The Argument Business

Paradoxically, perhaps, I have argued against arguing to win. Yet someone will ask, "How, if the apologist's business is to argue, can he help but argue to win? Isn't that the point of arguing?" Well, yes and no. If you think you are right, you argue to convince others of the truth of what you believe. You try to agree on truth. People who say we should never argue might as well say we should never try to overcome our differences. For coming to an agreement about matters of truth usually involves argument in one form or another. The apologist, then, should do his best to argue for the truth and to get others to agree with him.

The apologist's goal of agreement in the truth does not mean he wants to win at all costs. If the end is agreement or communion in the truth, the means cannot be to win the argument at the *expense* of truth. The apologist who genuinely argues for love of truth will want to lose an argument if winning it means moving further from the truth or embracing error. He will even be willing to let the other fellow think him less learned or knowledgeable if that means the other fellow will more readily accept the truth.

The apologist's work is certainly to argue, but only to explain and clarify, not to win. To achieve the proper goal of apologetical argument, our hearts must be right, that is, filled with charity. We must argue for the love of God, who is truth, and love of the person with whom we argue, not for the love of being right. Moreover, charity will help with *how* as well as *why* we argue.

Genuine apologetics involves dialogue, a true meeting of minds, not an exercise in mutual agnosticism that passes for dialogue in certain circles—you know, where nothing is certain except that the pope, the Church, or the Bible is wrong. Apologetics includes the kind of dialogue Paul VI discussed in his first encyclical, *Ecclesiam Suam* (Paths of the Church): a conversation that respects the intellect and freedom of the other person while challenging him to embrace the fullness of the truth. But I will say more on dialogue and charity in chapter 10, which discusses the habits of effective apologists.

7

Pride

We come at last to the final Deadly Sin of Catholic Apologetics, one that should be familiar enough to all of us. It is the great capital sin of the moral life, pride. Pride is undue love of oneself —undue because it conflicts with reality. You and I may not be as good as we think we are. We may love ourselves too much. We can distort the legitimate appreciation we should have of the good residing in us or in what we have accomplished. We can fail to see or acknowledge that good as God's gift. This is where the sin of pride enters.

Pride, for an apologist, involves thinking more highly of one's apologetical abilities than one should. The more effective an apologist someone becomes, the greater the temptation of seeing himself as "The Catholic Answer Man." "I have the arguments mastered," someone may think. "I don't have anything to learn." He may forget that it is the Holy Spirit, not his cleverly crafted arguments, who reaches minds and hearts and brings people to faith.

Seldom, of course, do any of us succumb to pride in such a manifest and gross fashion. For the typical Catholic apologist, the temptation is probably more subtle. Weary of attacks on his Catholic faith, and deeply appreciative of the richness of his Catholic heritage, he takes a certain legitimate pride in being a Catholic. For being a Catholic is a good thing. After all, do not we say in the baptismal liturgy, "This is the faith of the Church; we are proud to profess it in Christ Jesus"? Did not Paul "boast" of Christ?

The danger comes when we move from legitimate pride in being a Catholic to sinful pride. From recognizing our faith as a gift from God to thinking of it as a personal accomplishment or even a personal edge we have over others. For apologists, it can mean going from an authentic sense of accomplishment in the work to a boastful attitude: "Look at how many people I have converted! Look at how many debates I've won!"

Pride often leads to presumption. For the apologist, this can mean thinking himself capable of tackling any apologetical issue or answering any question, or that his particular approach to an issue is necessarily the right one. I do not mean simply succumbing to the First Deadly Sin of Catholic Apologetics, trying to prove too much. I mean reaching beyond one's abilities, in one's own strength, or assuming that knowing the arguments necessarily means one can present them effectively, in any situation, or better than anyone else.

Triumphalism

Pride can also involve an arrogant dismissiveness of others and their perspectives. To be sure, the Catholic apologist thinks Catholicism true. He even thinks it better than non-Catholic religions. Why settle for being a Catholic if another faith is superior? But that says nothing about the worth of the Catholic as a person, in comparison with his non-Catholic neighbor. Our Catholic faith is God's gift, not a personal accomplishment. Being Catholic does not mean we have nothing to learn from non-Catholics or that non-Catholics are, by definition, unintelligent for not having seen the truth of Catholicism.

A Catholic friend once belittled Calvinists as "mental midgets" because they believe in election and predestination. "How can any intelligent believer hold such things?" he gibed. Later, a Calvinist opponent showed him how Catholicism, too, affirms election and predestination, though not in the same way as Calvinism. The Calvinist went on (rightly) to argue that, with some important qualifications, the Thomistic view comes close to that of Calvinism. Since Thomas Aquinas was no mental midget, my friend had to eat humble pie. Calvinists are not so dumb after all, he admitted, even if, from the Catholic perspective, they are mistaken on some key issues.

I have seen this sort of thing among some cradle-Catholic apologists who have relatively little familiarity with the intricacies of Protestant theology. They simply presume that because Catholicism is true and, by implication, Protestantism is false (at least where it differs with Catholicism), Protestantism is unsophisticated and has nothing to say for itself. I remember one cradle-Catholic apologist, who once asserted that Protestants had no "real theologians," almost being floored by the erudition displayed by the then-Protestant, now-Orthodox Jaroslav Pelikan in his multivolume work, *The Christian Tradition*. I think it almost shook the Catholic apologist's faith. Only someone grossly ignorant of Protestantism or grossly arrogant about Catholicism, or both, could react so.

We converts from Protestantism, though far from ignorant of Protestant theology, can also succumb to pride when it comes to dealing with our former brethren. You see, we often feel that we have heard it all before. "Yes, I, *too*, used to think as you do," was how I once put it to a Protestant acquaintance. What I said was true, but there was more than a touch of superiority lurking behind my words. May God forgive me. How I must have driven the fellow further from the truth by my condescension!

One Protestant convert I know was so convinced of his ability to defend Catholicism that he claimed he could prove *any* Catholic belief or practice from the Bible alone! Think about the implication of that claim for a moment. In order for him to prove *any* Catholic belief or practice from the Bible alone, the Bible would have to be sufficient, in the Fundamentalist sense of the term. If every Catholic doctrine can be proved from the Bible, and the Bible alone, the Fundamentalists have been right about *sola scriptura* all along, even if they have been mistaken about the actual content of the Bible's teaching! Only my friend's arrogance kept him from seeing the irony of the point.

One form the apologist's pride can take is keeping a tally of how many converts he has made or, worse, how many non-Catholic opponents he (thinks he) has vanquished in argument. If pride is undue self-esteem—*pace* psychobabblers, too much self-esteem is a bad thing—then the man who puts a notch in his apologist's belt every time he makes a convert is in trouble. Someone once asked Archbishop Sheen how many converts he had made over the years. The usually good-natured Sheen said, stern-faced, "I don't keep count!"

Old-fashioned Catholic triumphalism can be another form of apologist pride. Triumphalism confuses the Church as the *beginning* (or seed) of the kingdom of God on earth with the fullness of the kingdom in the age to come. Consequently, triumphalist Catholics downplay or ignore real mistakes of Catholic leaders in history, lest the Church on earth be seen as anything less than the spotless, heavenly Bride of Christ. "Pope Alexander VI had four children," the anti-Catholic accuser asserts (to take an example from Frank Sheed). The triumphalist replies, "Oh no, only three were ever proved," or, "So what? Henry VIII had six wives," as if non-Catholic foibles absolve Catholic sins.

Here an apologist's humility can be helped by reading some early twentieth-century apologetics—that is, if he is disposed to learn. Many Catholic apologists of the last century took immense pleasure in gloating over Protestant disunity, in contrast to Catholicism's then-monolithic unity. "Ask a Protestant clergyman a question, and you get one answer. Ask another the same question, and you get a different answer," one writer triumphantly declared. "But ask any Catholic priest a question and you get the same answer, no matter whom you ask. That is the difference between the Protestant churches and the Catholic Church." Q.E.D.: Protestantism is false, Catholicism true.

Try that same experiment today and you will get very different results. The Protestant clergy is as divided as ever, but what of the Catholic clergy? Go to a traditional parish, and Msgr. Smith will tell you what the Church teaches, sure enough. But down at St. Miscellaneous Parish Community of Faith, where Fr. Gus says the clown Masses and empowers people to do as they please, who knows what you will hear. Is contraception a sin? The Church and Msgr. Smith answer, "Of course!" But Fr. Gus is not sure. "What do you want *me* to say? That's for *you* and *your* conscience to decide."

The old argument can still be salvaged because beneath the specific example is an enduring principle. Priests today who give you their ideas instead of what the Church teaches simply are not behaving as Catholics, for a Catholic—especially a priest—looks to the authentic teaching of the Magisterium, not his own private opinions. Indeed, he derives his beliefs from magisterial teaching. Fr. Gus, then, simply fails to follow "the Catholic rule of faith," as the old theology manuals put it, in formulating his reply. But every Catholic priest who *does* follow the Catholic rule of faith will give the same answer.

Protestant clergy, on the other hand, disagree among themselves. Perhaps, in a given instance, this results from ignoring or rejecting the Protestant rule of faith, the Bible alone. A Protestant minister may, for example, reject infant baptism because he no longer believes what the Bible says about original sin. He is like the priest who rejects the teaching of the Magisterium. Thus, the two examples cancel each other out. Then again, the Protestant minister may reject infant baptism because he is a Baptist and does not believe the Bible endorses it. He differs with his Lutheran, Anglican, and Presbyterian colleagues over the interpretation of the Bible, not because he rejects it as the rule of faith.

The point is, the old apologetics boasted about something it had no business boasting about—if it had any business boasting at all. The fact that *at the time* Catholic priests almost always answered according to Catholic teaching was no guarantee it would always be so. Perhaps no one could have anticipated the dissent and confusion that would follow Vatican II. Still, dissent and confusion among the clergy were not invented in 1965 or 1968. One has only to think back to the modernist controversy at the turn of the century or to Reformation-era clergy. Besides, the Church's unity does not guarantee that her priests will always teach what they should, any more than the Church's holiness guarantees priests will always live holy lives. The oneness of the Church does not vouchsafe a monolithic clergy, though the old apologetics sometimes sounds as if it did.

Apologetic Apologists

Although some dissident Catholics wrongly see *any* staunch affirmation of Catholicism as triumphalism, that does not mean apologists never fall into the real thing. Triumphalism is an unwillingness to acknowledge adequately that the Church, though holy, is also always in need of purification in her members (CCC 827). It is a subtle form of bravado masquerading as faith and zeal, a vice made out to be a virtue. And it is also immensely counterproductive for apologetics. Truthfulness about Catholic shortcomings is obligatory because truthfulness is obligatory. But there is also a practical benefit to us as apologists: if we are honest about sins committed by Catholics, even by popes and bishops—often in Christ's name—why should not non-Catholics believe us to be honest in other matters? But if we cannot admit unpleasant truths about Catholic history that everyone knows, then how likely is it non-Catholics will listen to us when we proclaim truths others dispute? We should not exaggerate Catholic sins, especially when so many today are willing to do that for us. But Catholics must acknowledge their sins, as John Paul II has repeatedly done. Honesty and repentance are two prerequisites for growth in the spiritual life, including the apologist's spiritual life.

John Paul II confessed the sins of other Catholics in history, not for himself. We, on the other hand, may need to confess our own sins. Apologists often ask the disgruntled former Catholic to forgive the priest who "drove him from the Church" or the Catholic family member who grievously wronged him. Sometimes we even apologize for these people. It is much harder, though, to ask forgiveness for what we ourselves have done, especially if we did it in the name of the truth.

8

Are the Seven Deadly Sins of Catholic Apologetics True Sins?

We have considered all seven of the Deadly Sins of Catholic Apologetics. Now what are we going to do about them? Before we can answer that, we must revisit another issue raised in the introduction: whether these "deadly sins" really are sins. Are we using the word "sins" as a metaphor for "mistake" or "error"? If we commit any of these deadly sins, should we confess them?

As I said in the introduction, one of the Seven Deadly Sins of Catholic Apologetics is obviously a bona fide sin—pride—at least in the sense used here. Whether it is grave matter for apologists who succumb to it—and therefore a matter of sacramental confession and absolution—is for the sinner and his confessor to decide. But what about the other apologetical "sins"? Are they, in any real sense, sins, whether grave or light?

Something is a sin, in the fullest sense, if 1) it is contrary to God's law, 2) we know it is wrong, and 3) we freely choose to do it (CCC 1857). Of course we can *think* something is wrong when it really is not. If we do it anyway, we are blameworthy for having sinned because we chose to do what we *thought* was wrong, even if what we did really was not. In that sense, an act can be compatible with God's law and yet we can be held accountable for having sinned by engaging in it.

But we are not talking about someone subjectively thinking the Seven Deadly Sins of Catholic Apologetics are wrong and committing them anyway. We are asking whether they are *really* wrong, in the moral sense. It is not simply a question of a counterproductive or less-effective action, or of a mistaken notion or wrong-headed idea; there must be a moral dimension to an action for it to be sinful. Furthermore, while culpability requires knowledge and consent, the action itself is *materially* sinful if it is contrary to God's law, regardless of whether we know it and consent to it as such. In the latter case, we may not be blameworthy for an action, but the action remains wrong in itself—contrary to God's will.

For the other six Deadly Sins of Catholic Apologetics to be true sins as such, therefore, they must be contrary to God's law, not merely bad ideas or ineffective techniques. Perhaps, if they are sins, we only now realize they are wrong or, having previously recognized that they are wrong, we are nonetheless so habituated to doing them that we do not act with full freedom. In other words, maybe we are not culpable or fully culpable. But the issue remains, "In what sense is sin involved?"

Here we should return to a distinction, mentioned in the introduction, between the directly sinful—something sinful per se, or what the moral theologians call "intrinsically evil"—and what is only indirectly sinful or perhaps sinful only in a certain context. I refer here to an act that is sinful under certain circumstances or that easily leads to acts sinful in themselves. Are any of the other Deadly Sins of Catholic Apologetics genuine sins (we have excluded pride), in either sense?

One thing is clear: they certainly have significant moral aspects. At least we can discern ways the moral law could come into play, even if indirectly, by engaging in such actions. For example, the Sixth Deadly Sin, trying to be King of the Apologetical Hill, often involves sins against truth. The drive to win at all costs, as we have seen, can lead to deliberate misrepresentation of the facts. That is a sin against the Eighth Commandment when, for instance, the truth about other people or what they believe is involved.

What about Deadly Sin Number Five, Not Distinguishing Enemies from Cobelligerents? A mistake or a sin? It depends on whether we realize we are aiming our apologetical firepower at an ally—or at least a cobelligerent—when we should be firing at someone else or not firing at all. All other things being equal, something is wrong when an apologist can only relate to non-Catholics by arguing with them or when an apologist spends his time arguing with, say, the Protestant neighbor on one side of the street while ignoring the atheist neighbor on the other side. Perhaps the apologist has a grudge against Protestantism or some other issue is at work.

One apologist I know always engages Muslims politely but comes with dagger drawn when talking to Evangelicals. Obviously, he has "issues." This is not to say that Evangelicals are always allies and Muslims always enemies, only that since we have far more in common with Evangelicals than Muslims, the former deserve to be dealt with at least as politely as the latter. Sin enters in to the extent that my friend deliberately mistreats Evangelicals as enemies, under circumstances in which they should be regarded as allies, and he knows it—or should. What may really be at work is plain old-fashioned bigotry. In any case, it is wrong.

Contentiousness—the Fourth Deadly Sin of Catholic Apologetics—resembles pride; most of us can see straightaway its link to sin. The contentious apologist is the apological equivalent of the barroom brawler, or apologetics bully. It is not just that he wants to win at all costs; it is that he is always *looking* for a fight. Of course, enjoying a good intellectual scuffle can be a matter of personality and disposition; it is not necessarily sinful. Many people who knew C. S. Lewis well have said that he liked a good battle of wits. G. K. Chesterton, too, debated at the drop of a hat or the downing of a pint—although a bit more good-naturedly than Lewis, by most reports.

But unchecked and wedded to insecurities, resentment, or bitterness—to name only a few things—the inclination to a good fight becomes sheer contentiousness, trying to do in the other guy by arguments. To the extent one realizes that it is wrong and wills it anyway, it becomes sin. Zeal in battling for the truth becomes zeal for crushing the enemy—at all costs. And where there is the desire to hurt or injure, we have a sin against charity.

The Third Deadly Sin of Catholic Apologetics, Confusing the Faith with One's Arguments for It, can also have a sinful aspect.

When we insist that our arguments be accepted as if they were the faith itself, we run a grave risk. Espousing our ideas as if they were the faith comes very close to espousing them *because* they are ours, regardless of the truth or even, perhaps, at the expense of truth. And *that* involves loving ourselves more than the truth, which can lead to a sin against the Eighth Commandment. It can also lead to the sin of heresy, asserting our own ideas in the face of what we know or reasonably suspect is God's word. Indeed, the word heresy itself comes from the Greek word *hairesis*, "choice." True heretics choose to put their own ideas or preferences ahead of the truth.

Against which of the commandments is the sin of heresy? Since it amounts to a rejection of God's word in preference to one's own ideas, heresy is a sin against faith and, therefore, against the First Commandment. The heretic sins, not only against truth in the abstract, but directly against the One who is truth, who can neither deceive nor be deceived. Thus, the Apologetical Sin of Confusing Our Faith with Our Arguments for It risks sinning against the First Commandment.

What about Deadly Sin Number Two—Reducing the Faith to Apologetics and Apologetics to Arguments? Well, if the Catholic faith is ultimately about communion with God—and it is— then anything that takes us away from the faith or reduces it to something it is not takes us away from God. It becomes a spiritual distraction. In this way, the misuse of apologetics can distract us from God himself. Thus, it can lead to a sin against the First Commandment. Our god becomes apologetics, not God; arguments, not the Almighty. We will have more to say about that when we talk about faith, hope, and charity in connection with apologetics and the habits of effective apologists.

The moral aspect is probably most indirect and therefore least obvious in the First Deadly Sin of Catholic Apologetics, Apologetical Gluttony. Crossing the line between what reason can prove on its own and what it cannot is not, per se, sinful, although it is per se erroneous. But refusing to observe the line, once you know where it is, can be sinful. It can involve arrogance on the part of the apologist, which is pride; and abuse of others, disrespect for them as free and thinking persons. If so, then, Apologetical Gluttony can involve a sin against charity.

There are more ways the Seven Deadly Sins of Catholic Apologetics can be truly sinful, but we cannot go into them here. Suffice it to say that we can see how true sin *can* be involved. And where sin is involved, repentance is necessary. Here we must underscore again that we are talking about more than honest mistakes or errors in technique; sin enters the picture when, with sufficient knowledge and consent, we do something wrong or something we think is wrong. But even when sin is not the issue, when we do not culpably do wrong, something must be done about the Seven Deadly Sins of Catholic Apologetics. Objectively speaking, they are contrary to God's will. The Catholic apologist, then, will want to eliminate them from his life. But how? We now turn to that subject.

9

What to Do about Them

Moral theologians say that one way to overcome a sinful habit is to develop the opposite virtue or habit. Are you proud? Cultivate humility. Lustful? Work on chastity. In a sense, such advice is obvious, as is the advice I am going to give about overcoming the Seven Deadly Sins of Catholic Apologetics. To overcome them, we must develop the opposite virtues or habits. In this chapter and the next, we will consider the Habits of Effective Apologists, habits that can help us avoid and overcome the Seven Deadly Sins of Catholic Apologetics.

Effective Apologists

What do I mean by an effective apologist? It is easier to say what I do not mean: I do not mean someone who is necessarily successful in the tally-of-converts sense. Jesus was not successful in that sense, at least not immediately. Three years of miracles, signs, and wonders garnered only a hundred and twenty disciples in the Upper Room awaiting Pentecost.

But Jesus was successful in another sense: he did what the Father wanted. On the cross he declared, "It is finished" (John 19:30), meaning that he had accomplished the work the Father gave him (John 4:34, 5:36, 17:4). The effective apologist, the truly successful apologist, is one who does the Father's will. To recall Mother Teresa's oft-repeated saying, God does not call us to be successful, only faithful. Fidelity is really the only kind of success God is interested in.

The effective apologist, then, is not worried about how many converts he makes. Someone can make many converts but still be unfaithful as a disciple. He may use methods unworthy of a true disciple or act from a wrong motive, such as vainglory. If he still wins converts, we should not be surprised; God uses whatever instruments he pleases, even inadequate ones. Besides, who among us, in the final analysis, is adequate? Do we really want the results of our apologetics tied to our personal sanctity?

Remember Sheed's story of the fornicating apologist? Despite the man's personal sinfulness, he defended the faith well; the truth has a power of its own, and God's Spirit is not limited by our moral failings. Sheed's example echoes a statement of the imprisoned Paul, who wrote of those who preached Christ from impure motives:

> Some indeed preach Christ from envy and rivalry, but others from good will. The latter do it out of love, knowing that I am put here for the defense of the gospel; the former proclaim Christ out of partisanship, not sincerely but thinking to afflict me in my imprisonment. What then? Only that in every way, whether in pretense or in truth, Christ is proclaimed; and in that I rejoice (Phil. 1:15–18).

Another reason not to worry about "success": there is no way to guarantee we will make x-number of converts. We can do things to minimize our chances of failure or maximize the likelihood of success. We can avoid making mistakes and use all human means of presenting a compelling image of the Catholic faith. But since conversion is ultimately the work of God and the grace-enabled free cooperation of man, we cannot guarantee success. So if you have just purchased the ten-tape series, *Seven Ways to Guarantee Conversion in Ten Easy Steps*, get a refund. You have been scammed.

The effective apologist, then, is the faithful apologist, one who does the Father's will without regard to consequences or score-keeping. But what specifically does that mean? It means acting according to God's purpose, with the right goal in mind and utilizing as best we can the appropriate means of attaining the goal. Let us consider those two things, the right goal and the appropriate means.

The first thing to note is that we can have one without the other. Our goal may be right—to help bring people into communion with God through the life of the Catholic faith. That is, after all, the bottom line of the Church's mission, even if apologists do this through defending the faith and answering objections. But the means we use to attain that goal may still be wrong. For example, an apologist may deliberately misuse the Bible or misrepresent the facts of Church history to suit his argument, manipulate people by means of rhetorical techniques, or employ sophisticated arguments to dodge real problems.

At the same time, an apologist may use correct methods but have the wrong goal. He may be out to win an argument, impress people with his brilliance, or overcome his own insecurities or lack of genuine faith. If he is a convert, he may be striking back at former coreligionists who hurt or offended him, or at family members. Any number of wrong motives can enter in. That the apologist more or less says or does the right things, then, does not guarantee he is truly an effective, that is, faithful, apologist.

Proper goal and means, then, are crucial, but there is a third necessary element: the effective apologist must be competent. He must know the faith and know how to defend it. It will not help much, even if his heart is in the right place and his method sound, if he does not know what he is talking about. That does not mean he must be "the Catholic Answer Man." The effective apologist need not be omniscient, but a basic level of apologetics knowledge is required, and there is no getting around it. We will return to that point shortly.

What Do We Mean by Habits?

So much for "effective." What about "habits"? What do we mean by "the habits of an effective apologist"? A habit is a tendency of behavior usually acquired through repeated actions. We usually have a habit because we have repeatedly performed certain actions. The habit now allows or inclines us to act, in a certain way, promptly and easily. The action becomes "second nature" to us. In the moral life, habits of acting badly—acting toward the wrong end or using the wrong means—are called vices. Habits of acting toward the proper end and using the proper means are called virtues.

Because the habits of effective apologists have significant moral aspects to them and important real goods associated with them— at least indirectly, as do the Seven Deadly Sins of Catholic Apologetics—we may speak of them as virtues, in a qualified sense. Some of them, as we shall see, are more obviously virtues, just as, in reference to the Seven Deadly Sins of Catholic Apologetics, pride is obviously a vice in the moral sense. Other apologetical virtues are more indirectly morally virtuous, insofar as we freely undertake the goal of apologetics and these virtues, or good habits, help us attain the goal.

Developing good habits requires patience as well as experience, the actual doing of something. For the latter there simply is no substitute. This is true whether you are acquiring the physical skills of bike riding or the evangelical and intellectual habits of apologetics. Sheed recounts the story of his dealings with a famous theologian. Toward the end of the man's career, Sheed convinced him to do some street-corner teaching for the Catholic Evidence Guild. At first, the theologian was practically unintelligible to the audience, but after some experience and practice of answering hecklers and having to hold an audience, he became an extremely lucid teacher of the faith. Sheed wondered what would have happened if the man had done street teaching at the beginning of his career rather than at the end.

Having clarified what we mean by effective apologists and by habits, we are in a better position to consider the topic of chapter 10, the Seven Habits of Effective Apologists. As we shall see, the list of these habits is by no means exhaustive, but it is difficult to imagine a consistently effective apologist who lacks any one of them.

Seven Habits of Effective Apologists

The better part of this book has been devoted to the Seven Deadly Sins of Catholic Apologetics; we could very well dedicate the better part of another book, or indeed a whole book, to Seven Habits of Effective Apologists. Nevertheless, I have decided to examine the habits of effective apologists in a single, final chapter because I think it unfair to diagnose the disease without saying something about the cure.

Unlike the above-mentioned deadly sins, on which I am expert from their prevalence in my own life, I claim no expert knowledge of the Seven Habits of Effective Apologists, except perhaps by a sort of *via negativa*. Whatever wisdom the reader finds herein comes from the sources I have consulted, not from an examination of my own accomplishments as an apologist.

As with the seven deadly sins, the number of positive habits is not set in stone. It might have been six or nine, with this habit added or that subsumed under another. Furthermore, the list is not obscure. The habits of effective apologists are straightforward: prayer, study, dialogue, clarity, faith, hope, and charity. The apologist who has mastered these things will certainly be effective, whatever other deficiencies he has or skills he needs to acquire.

1. Prayer

The essence of prayer, as every well-instructed Catholic knows, is the lifting of the mind and heart to God (CCC 2559). Every Christian must pray, but prayer is especially important for the apologist. He must have the habit of it. Sheed says somewhere that the theologian who does not believe is like the gourmet chef who does not eat: he knows a lot about the subject matter of his expertise, but has never experienced its reality. We could say the same of the apologist who does not pray.

Apologetics is very much about prayer. For apologetics is the business of defending the faith so that people can enter most fully into communion with God, who is truth. Prayer is the earthly form of that communion (CCC 2565); hence prayer is, in a sense, an important goal of apologetics. Apologetics should help bring people to prayer by disposing them to the grace of faith if they are unbelievers, opening them to the fullness of God's word if they are non-Catholic believers, and strengthening them in faith if they are already Catholics.

For the apologist, too, prayer is essential. The faithful apologist defends the faith, as we said earlier, because he loves God and his truth, which implies he knows something of God and his truth. As it would be a strange God who would be loved better for being known less, to paraphrase Sheed, so too would it be a strange God who would be known better for being conversed with less. Prayer, as conversation with God, leads to a deeper knowledge of God and the things of God. In other words, to a better appreciation of who and what the apologist is defending.

Then, too, there are practical reasons for apologists to pray. Prayer can motivate us to engage in apologetics. As the apologist's own prayer life grows, so does his displeasure with anything contrary to God's will. God wills that all men be saved and come to the knowledge of the truth (1 Tim. 2:4). Error keeps people from the truth. The closer the apologist grows to God in prayer, the more intense his hatred of error and his desire that all men know the truth; the more intense his desire to use apologetics to help bring people to the truth.

Prayer can also help us as apologists to avoid the sin of pride, which, as we have seen, can tempt us to regard ourselves as the source and end of our apologetical endeavors. Prayer can help us acknowledge ourselves as wholly dependent on God, as recipients of his gifts and graces, rather than as our own sources of truth and light. That, in turn, links prayer to the theological virtue of hope, about which we will say more shortly. With respect to the end, or goal, of our apologetical endeavors, prayer can remind us that God's glory and man's sanctification are the ultimate concern of apologetics, not self-aggrandizement.

Finally, prayer works. Prayer can help the apologist be better at his work and help those with whom he engages in apologetics. The apologist should pray that he may worthily defend the faith. He should pray for those with whom he discusses the faith, for their illumination and guidance, for their receptivity to the truth of the gospel. It is unlikely that an apologist will have as his true goal the spiritual good of those with whom he engages in apologetics if he never prays for them.

How should an apologist pray? Like any other Catholic, of course, in expressions of adoration and praise, repentance, thanksgiving, and supplication (CCC 2626–2642), privately and publicly. Receiving the sacraments is a form of prayer, the sacred liturgy being preeminent among them, since the Eucharist is the greatest of prayers (CCC 2643). Apologists, then, should fully participate in the sacramental life of the Church, especially the Holy Sacrifice of the Mass.

The English street teacher and writer Maisie Ward used to say that the apologist who is not soaked in the Gospels is an anomaly. So, we might add, is the apologist who does not pray, and not merely occasionally, but as a habit, as a virtue. For if all Christians must pray without ceasing, as Paul writes (1 Thess. 5:17), how much more the apologist, whose needs are at least as great?

2. Study

Prayer is not enough; the apologist must also study. In chapter 9, we said the apologist must be competent. Competence requires study. And the study must be ongoing because we never wholly master the faith or the objections raised against it. There is always more to learn. Thus, we must acquire the *habit* of study—study of the Catholic faith and whatever opposes it.

THE SUBJECT MATTER

The apologist must study the Catholic faith, not merely as a body of abstract beliefs or theological opinions, but as living truths informing a way of life and a view of reality. Good theology books can help here, but above all else the apologist should immerse himself in Catholic teaching as it is found in the word of God, in Scripture and Tradition as interpreted by the teaching office of the Church. The apologist unfamiliar with the Bible will suffer when talking with non-Catholic Christians or quasi-Christian groups such as the Jehovah's Witnesses or Mormons, for whom the idiom of theology is the Bible. I have seen such people pushed further away from the Catholic Church simply because the Catholic apologist with whom they spoke did not know his Bible as well as he should have. The apologist may have been accurate enough in explaining what Catholics believe, but he failed to translate it into the language of his more biblically oriented discussion partners.

There are three main ways an apologist should study the Bible. First, there is the sort of devotional Bible reading we all should do—spiritual reading. This kind of reading is geared to the apologist's spiritual nourishment and growth as a disciple, not specifically as an apologist. Even so, spiritual reading of the Bible will help the apologist. It can, for example, be a potent means of overcoming part of the Second Deadly Sin of Catholic Apologetics, reducing the Christian life to apologetics.

Then there is scholarly reading of the Bible. Most apologists, it is true, are not biblical scholars. Nevertheless, apologists operate in the world of theology and theological scholarship, so they should have some acquaintance with biblical scholarship as well as with the systematic theologian's reading of Scripture. I say "biblical scholarship" and the "systematic theologian's reading of Scripture" because the two are not necessarily the same. Biblical scholarship tries to get at what the text says and means, while the systematic theologian uses the Bible and biblical scholarship's findings to understand, distinguish, and finally synthesize into a coherent system the various elements of revelation. These tasks are related but distinct. The apologist, though not necessarily a theologian in a formal sense, nevertheless should be informed about both uses of Scripture.

For example, many contemporary Protestant biblical scholars argue that Paul's teaching against "the works of the Law" should not be read, as it often has been by Protestants in the past, through the lens of the Reformation debate over faith and works. These scholars insist that Paul's teaching concerns the uselessness of Old Covenant "identity markers," such as circumcision and the dietary laws, as grounds for justification before God, not whether works of Christian obedience are necessary for salvation. Whether this reading of Paul is entirely correct, or whether it will long endure, remains to be seen. There are fads among scholars as among fashion designers. The point is, Catholic apologists should be aware of such developments in biblical scholarship so that they can respond accordingly.

Finally, there is a specifically apologetical use of Scripture, which requires a certain kind of reading. For example, the apologist must know which texts support Catholic doctrine; he must also know which ones are used to attack it. He must know *how* these texts are used and be able to walk someone through various passages to support or defend Catholic beliefs. This last way of reading the Bible is distinct from the scholarly reading but must be informed by it. It does no good to build an argument for a Catholic tenet upon a text if the text does not mean what the apologist thinks or claims it does. In such a situation, the apologist's use of the Bible degenerates into proof-texting, in the pejorative sense. The maxim "A text taken out of context is a pretext" applies to Catholic apologists as well as to anti-Catholic polemicists.

Yet knowing the Bible is not enough. For one thing, doctrine has developed over the centuries beyond its inscripturated form. The Bible did not spell everything out as precisely as the Church's later needs required. Not everything Christians ought to believe *can* be deduced from the Bible alone, apart from Tradition. Even on the so-called one-source view of revelation, which posits Scripture's material sufficiency, we cannot jump from the New Testament to Vatican II in one bound. Something distinct from but not antithetical or heteronomous to the Bible is needed: Tradition.

Tradition includes, of course, the Fathers of the Church. Although most apologists readily turn to them to help make the case for Catholicism, it will not do to have only a vague sense that the Fathers taught Catholic doctrine. They did, of course, but in a more primitive form. We cannot expect to find in the Fathers a full-blown understanding of, say, the Petrine office or Mariology. Apologists who speak as if we can are either uninformed or they are oversimplifying to the point of deception. They are also seriously counterproductive. Sooner or later they will be caught out.

The apologist must also study what the Magisterium teaches. It is not enough to read books of theology, as vital as that can be. The apologist must know the *documents* of the Magisterium. Unfortunately, I have known Catholic apologists who have never bothered to open the sixteen documents of Vatican II. Their argument is that they do not really need to. "After all," they say, "the faith doesn't change."

There is a sense in which they are correct. The Church never presents as dogma anything contrary to what she has definitively taught in the past. Yet dogmas do develop. Earlier formulations can be refined, and certainly differences of time, place, and temperament can influence how the faith is presented. The Magisterium has a certain responsibility to read "the signs of the times" and to proclaim the ancient faith accordingly. The apologist who does not bother to read magisterial documents, especially recent ones, risks giving the right answer in the wrong way. By preferring his own ideas, he also risks presumptuously dismissing the discernment of his sacred pastors regarding the mission of the Church today.[1]

---

[1] When I underscore the need to read magisterial documents, I mean read them for more than proof texts. If some apologists virtually ignore the doc-

In addition to the faith of the Church, whether expressed in Scripture, Tradition, or the teaching of the Magisterium, apologists should also study the beliefs of non-Catholics. We must understand their thinking, their mindset, their worldview, if we are going to communicate with them. Here care must be taken. Unfortunately, as we have seen, some Catholics caricature non-Catholics. They may fail in charity or merely succumb to the convenience of oversimplifying things. Then, too, some apologists are simply ignorant of what non-Catholics really believe because they have not taken the time to find out. This also applies to non-Catholic arguments against the Catholic faith. Real non-Catholic objections, not straw men, should get our attention.

Thus far we have considered the content of apologetics as an object of study. There is also the question of method. We must study technique. We must learn how to defend the faith, not merely what the arguments are. Why is this important? As we have seen, apologetics has objective and subjective aspects. The content is part of the objective aspect. Method concerns the subjective aspect—how effectively to defend the faith with *this* person, given his background, concerns, and frame of mind.

Method includes logical and psychological elements of the subject. Logic, which focuses on correct thinking, is obviously crucial to argumentation. The apologist should study the principles of logic, and be keenly aware of the key logical errors, or fallacies. Because argumentation is a major aspect of apologetics, it is important to know when an argument leads us to the truth and when it only appears to do so. This knowledge allows apologists to avoid framing erroneous arguments and to detect them in the reasoning of others.

Logical elements are only part of the mix; psychological factors also enter in. What sorts of things make it psychologically diffi-

---

uments of Vatican II, others use them only as an arsenal for arguments. The texts must first be read in context, in the spirit in which they were written. Only after their message has been properly assimilated should the documents of Vatican II be used in apologetics.

cult for a person to follow an argument or accept Catholic truth? Apologetics is a person-specific endeavor, so we cannot give an all-encompassing answer to the question. Factors such as emotions, experiences, family background, and even ethnic prejudices can create obstacles to faith. Apologists should learn how to recognize such factors and develop strategies to work around them.

The Danger of Study

Study, then, is important, yet dangers accompany it. Regarding the discipline of the higher faculties, spiritual writers often refer to the intellectual defect of curiosity. Most of us consider curiosity a good thing, so it may seem odd to call it an intellectual defect. But here curiosity means the tendency or impulse to seek too eagerly knowledge of things that delight or interest us at the expense of what we *need* to know.

All of us have a finite amount of time, so we must use it wisely. That includes the time we commit to learning—even to learning about apologetics. The apologist should study what he needs to know before he studies what he likes. Of course, it is wonderful when the two things coincide. But what if they do not? What if the apologist is engrossed in the latest Michael O'Brien novel when he should be working through a chapter of the Bible, the *Summa Theologica* or the latest papal encyclical? Even within the field of apologetics, suppose an apologist is busy working on some obscure point because it interests him—arguments against papal primacy based on conciliarism from 1414 to 1517, or whatever —while neglecting the intellectual work that would make him a more well-rounded and useful apologist. Curiosity can kill the apologist as well as the cat.

Beyond our general responsibilities as Catholics, we are not obliged to study apologetics at all. Even if we think we are, a certain amount of reading can be properly recreational. But anyone who chooses to be an apologist in a serious way, whether professionally or as an avocation, assumes a certain obligation to do his best at it. We are, after all, talking about defending the Catholic faith. Someone who does not bother to study the subject broadly or systematically but wants to enter the apologetical fray in a serious way risks bringing ridicule upon himself and upon the faith. Better that he give up apologetics and study Portuguese or take up Tae Kwon Do as a hobby.

Another danger of study is getting in over one's head. This is a danger of theology in general. Not everyone's faith is firm enough to endure the systematic analysis and, in a certain sense, critical scrutiny that theological study entails. Someone who thinks the case for Catholic doctrine is in all respects plain and simple is riding for a fall if he studies the issues in depth. He may face temptations against the truth that he is not ready to meet. The same applies to the branch of theology called apologetics—only more so. In apologetics, one has to look at arguments against the faith, assess their relative strengths, and ask oneself, "Do I really have solid, rational grounds for what I say about this doctrine or that?" Questions such as those can challenge one's faith. They require discerning whether one is adequately prepared, as a believer, to engage in apologetics.

Meditation

The last thing to discuss under the rubric of study does not strictly belong there, but we needed to discuss study first in order to consider it adequately. I have thus placed it at the end of this section on study rather than under prayer, where it really belongs. The final topic, meditation, includes some of the same elements as study, although it is really a form of prayer. Meditation should be part of the apologist's habit of prayer and should draw on the fruit of his study.

How does meditation differ from study? Mainly in its purpose, or end. Like study, meditation has an intellectual aspect, understanding supernatural truths. But meditation has an additional purpose: to arouse love in the will in response to the truth understood by the intellect. It is the response of love that makes meditation a form of prayer.

Spiritual writers present different methods of meditation, although the basic structure is the same. Ignatian meditation proposes three stages: preparation, the body of the meditation, and a conclusion. In preparation, one makes acts of faith and reverence, prays for grace to meditate well, and asks for special graces regarding the specific meditation. In the body of the meditation, one recalls what is to be meditated on, reflects on it, thinks of its practical applications, tries to arouse devout feelings and affections about it, and then makes specific, practical resolutions. The conclusion involves talking to God about what one has meditated upon and offering a vocal prayer.

Apologists can use this procedure or similar ones. Not that the only form of meditative prayer an apologist uses should concern his work; meditation, like other forms of prayer, should be part of his general Christian life. Like the theologian, the apologist can be aided in his love for God and appreciation of God's truth through meditative prayer. Meditation should not become an excuse for running through arguments and ideas in the apologist's mind *instead* of praying. My friend's use of the Mass as an opportunity to devise arguments for the Real Presence is an example of that mistake. At the same time, it would be an intolerable disconnect in an apologist's spiritual life if he never prayerfully reflected on the truths he seeks to defend or the arguments he frames.

3. Dialogue

The Third Habit of Effective Apologists is dialogue. Dialogue here does not mean an occasional conversation with someone you disagree with but a habitual inclination to discuss—truly discuss—apologetics issues. Dialogue puts into practice what the apologist learns through study. It is one thing to formulate arguments on one's own, another to present them to someone who can argue back. The give and take of dialogue can help the apologist find weaknesses in his own arguments and understand the real issues dividing people.

This is dialogue in the full-blooded sense of the term, not—

as was said in a previous chapter—the anemic quest for the ever-elusive truth or a theological going-along-to-get-along. The apologist is not agnostic about the topic of dialogue; nor should he pretend he does not think his view is right—at least more right than other options. That would be dishonest. The apologist will benefit from dialogue, but not in that way.

Dialogue is the means by which a truth living in one mind becomes a truth living in another. It involves listening as well as speaking, receiving and giving. The apologist who dialogues with a non-Catholic should listen to what the non-Catholic's faith means to him, as well as present arguments for Catholic beliefs. He should take the time to hear what his non-Catholic discussion partner says, to understand the non-Catholic's worldview and the full force of his objections before responding to them. The key to dialogue is for both participants to understand one another, where they agree, where they disagree, and why.

I have said that dialogue can help the apologist do a better job of defending the faith. But the main reason apologists should acquire the habit of it is not merely that it is an effective technique; dialogue is fundamental to apologetics, basic to its very essence. The apologist who rejects dialogue rejects more than a useful tool or technique: he really rejects apologetics itself. This is because dialogue is necessary in order to do justice to the way human beings arrive at truth, especially the truth about God and what he has revealed. Indeed, God himself has dialogued with man. The whole story of God's revelation and man's response is a kind of dialogue.

In his first encyclical, *Ecclesiam Suam*, Paul VI identified dialogue as one of three attitudes the Church must have, especially today (13–14, 58). To explain what he meant, the Holy Father took as his model the "dialogue" between God and man in salvation history, which he dubbed "the dialogue of salvation" (70–77). He identified a number of elements of the dialogue of salvation that should also characterize the Church's dialogue with the world. We can apply these elements to the dialogue of apologetics as well.

First, noted Paul VI, God took the initiative with man. The

Church, then, should "take the initiative in extending to man this same dialogue, without waiting to be summoned to it" (72). Similarly, the apologist should take the initiative to engage the non-Catholic, to strike up a conversation aimed at understanding the other, not merely as entrée to an argument (although there is a place for that) or a response to attacks or objections.

Second, the dialogue of salvation began with charity, with God's goodness and love. Thus, Paul VI wrote, "nothing but fervent and unselfish love should motivate our dialogue" (73). We will discuss charity in more detail shortly. The point here is that an apologist's dialogue must be motivated by, and carried out in, charity, not by the thrill of the apologetical kill or by the desire to show off or win the argument.

Third, God did not force himself on man in the dialogue of salvation. Rather, he appealed through love, which left man free to accept or reject it. "Even the number of miracles and their demonstrative power," according to Paul VI, "were adapted to the spiritual needs and dispositions of the recipients, in order that their free consent to the divine revelation might be facilitated, without, however, their losing the merit involved in such a consent" (75). The Holy Father here repudiated physical coercion in the Church's mission, arguing that the Church should use "legitimate means of human education, of interior persuasion, of ordinary conversation" (75). For the apologist, physical compulsion is not an issue, but logical or psychological compulsion can be. The apologist is neither a propagandist, in the pejorative sense, nor a proselytizer. He is a kind of evangelist or an evangelist's collaborator, answering objections so that people can freely and intelligently embrace the fullness of the gospel message. That means he must use methods compatible with the free acceptance of that message. If the miracles of Jesus left room for free consent or rejection, then so must the dialogue of the apologist.

Fourth, the dialogue of salvation was aimed at all men. Paul VI concluded from this that the Church should be willing to dialogue with everyone, rejecting only those who absolutely repudiate dialogue with the Church or only pretend to accept it. In the dialogue of apologetics, we should also aim to speak with all men, not merely those with whom we find it easiest to argue—usually Fundamentalists and Evangelicals.

Fifth, the dialogue of salvation moved people toward the truth gradually, in successive advances. The Church's dialogue with the world should do the same, as should the apologist's dialogue with non-Catholics. Errors and sins of the past, differences in world-view, terminology, and concerns, even the individual limitations of our dialogue partners or of ourselves as apologists often mean progress must be gradual and successive. The recent Lutheran-Catholic *Joint Declaration on Justification* is an example of the gradual and successive approach. The agreement does not cover the whole of the doctrine of justification, much less the whole of the Christian faith. It focuses on a very specific slice of the subject. Better to digest things well one slice at a time than to bite off more than we can chew.

Those are what Paul VI called "elements of dialogue." He also described "characteristics of dialogue": clarity, meekness, trust, pedagogical prudence, union of truth and charity. Clarity and the union of truth and charity we will consider in themselves as habits of effective apologists. Meekness, trust, and pedagogical prudence we should say something about here.

Meekness does not mean hanging a sign on your forehead that reads "Doormat." *Meekness*, as in "The meek shall inherit the earth" (cf. Matt. 5:5), is a form of temperance. It is the virtue by which we moderate anger or resentment. It is also a much-needed quality in dialogue, especially apologetical dialogue. According to Paul VI, "The dialogue is not proud, it is not bitter, it is not offensive. Its authority is intrinsic to the truth it explains, to the charity it communicates, to the example it proposes; it is not a command, it is not an imposition. It is peaceful; it avoids violent methods; it is patient; it is generous" (ES 81). We need to reread that and examine our consciences. I suspect most of us apologists come up short on that score, at least some of the time.

Trust is also a characteristic of dialogue done right. Dialogue participants must trust one another to be honest and open-minded, to listen as well as speak. If there is no basic trust between or among dialogue participants, little genuine understanding will result. "But what if you just can't trust your dialogue partners?" someone may object. Then why waste time talking with them? Find someone you can trust and talk to him.

The last of Paul VI's characteristics of dialogue to be considered here is pedagogical prudence. Echoing Thomas Aquinas, Paul VI stressed that dialogue must be adapted to the nature of the interlocutor and the factual circumstances of the dialogue (78). We must appreciate the psychological and moral circumstances of the listener (81), so that Catholic dialogue participants can adapt themselves and their message, "lest we be displeasing and incomprehensible" to those with whom we dialogue.

For example, the apologist should understand that Protestants often mean by faith more than "the supernatural assent of the intellect to God and what he reveals, on the authority of God who reveals," which is more or less how traditional Catholic theology has understood the term. The apologist should adapt his own discussion of the subject to take into account a different use of the word as well as a different understanding of faith. Another example is the common Muslim misunderstanding that the Christian belief in the Trinity implies polytheism. The Christian apologist who cavalierly talks about the divinity of Jesus may wind up driving a Muslim further from the truth. Instead, he must show not that Jesus is not *another* God *in addition* to the Father, but that they are the *same* God. The Christian apologist must insist that Christians are as monotheistic as Muslims because Christianity asserts the fundamental and indivisible unity of the divine nature, whatever else Christians may believe about the three Persons in the one God.

A final point about dialogue: it can help foster what has been called "ecumenical apologetics." Ecumenical apologetics is not apologetics engaged in by ecumenists; it is a way of engaging in Catholic apologetics. It begins with the elements of truth in non-Catholic religions and tries to show that the full, integral expression of those truths is found in Catholicism. This is the kind of apologetics Louis Bouyer practiced over fifty years ago in *The Spirit and Forms of Protestantism*. Bouyer argued that some of the main points of Protestantism—the supremacy of the word of God and the gratuitousness of salvation—are Catholic and that the Catholic Church is necessary for the full flowering of these truths. Ecumenical apologetics does not start out with "You're wrong, and let me show you where you went astray." It begins with something like this: "What do we agree about? Let's look at that. Then you can tell me where you think the Catholic Church is off the mark or where you have problems with it. Then I'll tell you why I think the Church is correct and where it seems to me you may be missing something."

4. Clarity

As noted a moment ago, Paul VI identified clarity as one of the characteristics of genuine dialogue (ES 81). You cannot get very far in a conversation if you are not clear about what you mean. Clarity is required in at least two areas of theological discussion. First, regarding where we agree with others. As Paul VI noted, "A man must first be understood; and, where he merits it, agreed with" (87). Some differences are merely terminological. Catholics may not commonly use the expression "accepting Jesus as one's personal Lord and savior," for example, but there is nothing un-Catholic about the basic idea it expresses.

But we must also be clear about real differences. "The apostle's art," wrote Paul VI, "is a risky one. The desire to come together as brothers must not lead to a watering down or subtracting from the truth." He went on to note, "An immoderate desire to make peace and sink differences at all costs is, fundamentally, a kind of skepticism about the power and content of the word of God we desire to preach" (88).

In the long run, it does no good to paper over differences; it is actually harmful. As we saw in chapter 5, Vatican II's Decree on Ecumenism declares that "Catholic belief must be explained more profoundly and precisely, in such a way and in such terms that our separated brethren can also really understand it" (*Unitatis Redintegratio* 11). But that statement is preceded by another one: "Nothing is so foreign to the spirit of ecumenism as a false irenicism which harms the purity of Catholic doctrine and obscures its genuine and certain meaning" (ibid.). If one goal of dialogue is unity, or communion in the truth, then ambiguity about differences ultimately frustrates that goal. Agreement then becomes only apparent, not real.

That is clarity in speaking; there is also clarity in thinking. Usually the latter precedes the former, although the unclear thinker makes at least one thing clear when he speaks: he has only a foggy idea of what he is talking about. A man who can not explain something clearly does not have a firm grasp of the subject. There is a close correlation between one's ability to explain something and one's understanding of it. At least it seems fair to say that the first step to explaining something clearly to others is to have a clear grasp of it yourself. That stipulation should lead us all back to ongoing study and meditation.

5. Faith

We come now to the last three habits of effective apologists considered in this chapter, the theological virtues. Is it trite to include them among the habits of effective apologists? It seems to go without saying that apologists should have these virtues, as indeed all Catholics should. Nevertheless, they are on the list for good reason. The practice of apologetics carries with it certain occupational hazards with respect to faith, hope, and charity.

Apologists can miss the point of believing by embracing "the faith" as a set of propositions or even as a mere philosophy of life. We have already seen that genuine faith entails believing on the authority of God who reveals rather than on the strength of our arguments for belief. Although arguments may lead to motives of credibility, they are not themselves *what* we believe or even, ultimately, *why* we believe. When an argument leads us to conclude that a particular dogma of the faith is true, our certainty of its truth, as a matter of faith, rests on God's authority, not the force of the argument. We are not, then, believing a set of conclusions, no matter how cogently argued. We are saying yes to God and to what he has revealed.

Even when we truly believe what God has revealed, we can still miss the point of it. To think certain propositions true because they follow from sound arguments is one thing. To believe certain propositions true because we *believe* God has revealed them is something else. Yet even when we as apologists *believe* the truths of the faith, it still is not enough. As important as faith is, it must still be completed, or formed, by charity. To understand that issue properly, we should back up a bit.

When we believe the dogmas of the faith, we in some sense touch the realities they express (CCC 170). On this point, the *Catechism* quotes Thomas Aquinas: "The believer's act [of faith] does not terminate in the propositions, but in the realities [which they express]" (ibid.). When we believe, then, we are in contact with certain realities, not merely propositions about them. There is a certain analogy here to objects of thought, such as truth, justice, beauty, and wisdom. We can distinguish the ideas *by which* we know these realities from the realities themselves. It is a subtle philosophical point, but it has an application to what we believe as Catholics.[2]

Thus, when it comes to truths of the faith, we can distinguish

---

[2] This distinction comes from traditional Thomistic teaching regarding how and what we know and understand. We can distinguish an idea as that by which we know or understand from an idea as that which we know or understand. In the former sense, ideas are subjective. I have mine and you have yours. In the latter sense, ideas can have a quasi-objectivity for human beings in that you and I can, for example, both understand the idea of justice, as an object of thought. When we truly understand justice, we understand the same thing. I understand it by virtue of my idea of justice and you understand it by virtue of your idea of justice, but the idea of justice that we both will understand is the same. For a popular discussion of th' two senses of the word idea considered here, see Mortimer J. Adler's book *Ten Philosophical Mistakes*, Chapter 1, "Consciousness and Its Objects."

the *truths* we believe from the *propositions* that express what we believe. Even so, it is not enough that we go from propositions to the truths they express. In believing, we also submit ourselves to a person: Jesus Christ. Faith orients us to a person as well as to propositions or to truths expressed by those propositions. After all, in the act of faith we believe *what* we do (the truths of the faith) because of *whom* we believe (God, who reveals; or Jesus Christ, who fully reveals God to us). As John Paul II teaches,

> "To believe" means to accept and to acknowledge as true and cor-responding to reality the content of what is said, that is, the content of the words of another person (or even of more persons) by reason of his (or their) credibility. . . . So then by saying "I believe," we express at the same time a double reference—to the person and to the truth; to the truth in consideration of the person who enjoys special claims to credibility (General Audience, May 13, 1985; cf. CCC 177).

Because faith involves believing God's word on the authority of God who reveals, faith involves a submission to God—a sub-mission of the will, which is moved by grace, and of the intellect, which, moved by the will, assents to God's word. Christians sub-mit to God's Word in the person of Jesus. Thus, the act of faith itself is submission to the person of Jesus. But faith is complete only when we love Jesus, to whom we assent with faith. For only in charity is our submission to Jesus complete. Only when we love God do we come to the point or the purpose of believing him in the first place. Without charity, faith is still faith, but it is "dead faith" (cf. Jas. 2:26), unable of itself to complete our union with God: "He who does not love does not know God; for God is love" (1 John 4:8). And as Paul writes, "If I have all faith, so as to remove mountains, but have not love, I am nothing" (1 Cor. 13:2).

In chapters 1 and 3, we stressed the practical reality of faith with respect to apologetics. We said that some things—the truths of revelation that are above reason—require faith if we are to affirm them at all. We also saw that if we confuse our arguments for the faith with the faith itself, our faith can falter when our arguments do. Now we should add another element: when someone raises an objection to Catholic belief that appears to us unanswerable, the virtue of faith can sustain us. Our assent to Catholic dogmas does not rest on the force of argument anyway; it rests on the authority of God who reveals—on faith, in other words. So when the force of the particular argument for the faith is undermined, or appears to have been, if our faith is truly in God who reveals, there should be no real problem. C. S. Lewis called this "obstinacy in belief."

Part of the difficulty some apologists have here stems from the fact that faith involves entrusting. By faith we entrust ourselves to God with respect to the truth. When we argue for a certain truth, we can easily slip into entrusting ourselves to our own arguments, our own intellectual abilities. In this way, we retain control of the situation (or so it appears to us) because we control our arguments, which we see as the products of our reasoning powers. Unfortunately, some apologists are so used to calling the shots and framing the arguments that they may fear letting go and just believing God. While believing should be reasonable, not blind, it is still believing, not arguing or proving.

6. Hope

The Sixth Habit of Effective Apologists is the theological virtue of hope. We already mentioned it in connection with prayer: turning to God in dependence on him in prayer is tied to hope. Now we consider it directly, in itself.

Hope is the virtue by which we desire God as our highest good and firmly expect to enjoy eternal life with him, trusting and relying on him to provide us with the necessary means (CCC 1817, 2090). Hope is the virtue of placing our confidence in God because he is all-good and all-powerful. Since he is all-good, he wants to save us. Since he is all-powerful, he can accomplish what he wants.

Of course, apologetics is not salvific in the same way as, say, receiving the Holy Eucharist or going to confession. But engaging in apologetics can contribute to our salvation because, if pursued rightly, it can bring us closer to God. In that sense, in a secondary way, apologetics can be an object of hope. If we can hope even for earthly goods to the degree they are necessary or helpful to our spiritual perfection, we can certainly hope for and rely on God's aid when it comes to engaging in apologetics. That is, we can hope in God, relying on him to help us engage in apologetics properly, in a way that brings us closer to him and, therefore, helps us grow in holiness. Not only *can* we hope in God in apologetics, we *must*. We can plant the seed and water it, but it is God who gives the increase, even in apologetical argument.

Spiritual writers point to two main sins against hope, presumption and despair. Presumption expects God to save us, without our willingness to use the means he has established. We sin by presumption when we judge ourselves capable of pleasing God by our own powers or when we think that God's goodness will save us regardless of what we do or do not do (CCC 2090). Despair, by contrast, either denies that God can save us even if we use the means he has given us, or it denies that he wants to save us (CCC 2091). In this sense, despair is more than an emotional state; it is an act of the will to disregard God's power and goodness.

How do presumption and despair relate to apologetics? The apologist can sin by presumption in a number of ways. He may, for example, presume he can do something that cannot be done, such as to prove a truth of revelation unknowable from unaided reason (which I have called the First Deadly Sin of Catholic Apologetics). Perhaps he thinks so highly of his own abilities that he refuses to accept or acknowledge the limits of the human intellect or of any man's persuasive powers. Or perhaps he subtly convinces himself that his apologetics work will make up for any lapses in his personal sanctity—the Second Deadly Sin of Catholic Apologetics, reducing the Christian life to apologetics.

Likewise, the apologist can sin through despair. Should his faith falter, his hope in the power of God to bring people to the truth may also collapse. Such personal failures can lead him to despair of God's using him as an apologist, which in turn may lead him to despair of God altogether—of God's power, his goodness, or both.

How can we foster the virtue of hope in apologetical work? By meditating on what our hope is founded upon, the power and goodness of God, and on his promises to us. It is the power of God that converts hearts and minds. Our arguments are, at best, mere instruments he employs. Yet God has promised to be with his disciples when they present the truth, so even our poor abilities can, by his grace, bring others to the truth.

We also foster hope by making repeated acts of hope and by avoiding presumption and despair. We must not presume either that apologetics will save us or that God's love for us is measured by how successful we are in answering objections or winning converts. Nor should we presume on our abilities. Whatever we have, we have as God's gift. Whatever we achieve, we achieve by his gift as well.

In the final analysis, do we apologists really desire God, or do we just want to argue about him? If God is truly our desire above all things and if everything we do is done to his glory and as a means of being united to him, then our hope remains firm. We will not desire to prove more than we can or force the truth on others. We will rightly appreciate what God can do through apologetics in general and through us in particular. In short, we will realize that our hope is in the Lord, not in ourselves.

7. Charity

Finally we come to charity, the greatest of the theological virtues and indeed the "form of all virtues" (CCC 1827). Charity is the virtue by which we love God above all things for his own sake and love our neighbor as ourselves for love of God (CCC 1822). And as we saw in our discussion of faith, charity, or love of God, "forms" faith, bringing it to completion by uniting us completely to God.

Because charity orders us to God, when we engage in apologetics charitably, we do so for love of God. Because we love him, his truth, and his will, we share that truth with others. Because charity helps us to love the truth more than we love ourselves, it disposes us to subordinate our own ideas and our arguments *for* the truth *to* the truth itself. And because charity entails love of neighbor for the sake of our love of God, it motivates us to respond respectfully to those who object to the faith. Charity, then, helps the apologist to seek the right end and to use the right means of attaining it.

That last point is worth developing. Some apologists act as if they think it sufficient to have a charitable end in view—say, convincing a man of Catholic truth or defending the faith from attack. But if the means employed are uncharitable, incompatible with the love of God or the dignity of human beings, there is a problem. A charitable apologetical end does not justify uncharitable apologetical means.

In chapter 5, we discussed the Inquisition. We can be certain those saints who took part in or defended the Inquisition had a charitable goal in view, the salvation of souls. Yet the means the Inquisition sometimes employed—torture, for example—were incompatible with human dignity. Such means were irreconcilable with the real good of those subjected to the torture and, therefore, objectively speaking, contrary to charity. This is true regardless of the subjective inculpability of a particular inquisitor or defender of the Inquisition. The aforementioned saints did not see the problem of the means at the time because such methods were generally accepted and regarded as compatible with the good of the people subjected to them. If they had, they would no doubt have rejected such inappropriate means to the good end of helping people attain salvation.

Nowadays we need not worry about the Inquisition. But we still have to analyze our methods. Are they truly compatible with the love of God and the *real* good of the people we talk to? If not, then charity requires us to abandon them. For we cannot simultaneously will the good of another as an end while deliberately acting contrary to his good as a means—at least not if we really understand what we are doing.

For some readers, exhortations to charity may seem superflu-
ous, yet there are Catholic apologists who seriously say things such
as "Damn the heretics!" and "To hell with them!" and then pat
themselves on the back for their evangelical and apologetical zeal.
How can we square that attitude with charity? The short answer:
we cannot. If charity wills the good of another, taking delight
in his damnation hardly seems charitable. Perhaps those who say
such things do not really mean what they appear to mean. Perhaps
they merely take delight in God's justice being done, not in another person's misery. The distinction between the two attitudes,
however, is razor-thin, and razor-thin distinctions sometimes slice
up those unskilled in making them. Any of us can stumble or
fall in the charity department, but that is different from priding
ourselves—in the name of charity—on what is really a lack of
charity. That is dressing up our vices as virtues.

As apologists, we grow in charity by avoiding sin and by engaging in repeated acts of loving God and loving others for the
sake of our love of God. By "avoiding sin" I mean avoiding the
real thing—acts contrary to God's law. The Seven Deadly Sins
of Catholic Apologetics enter in here to the extent they involve
genuine sins. And when we sin as apologists, we should repent
of having offended God in our work, acknowledge our actions as
unworthy of God's service and the gifts he has bestowed on us,
and commit ourselves to conform our future efforts to his will.

Repeated acts of loving God depend on faith and reflection. We
must believe that God is worthy of all our love, worthy of being
loved above all things for his own sake. We must repeatedly reflect
on that fact and then resolve, by his grace, to value God above
all things, in our thoughts, words, and deeds—in our arguments
and debates, too.

Nor must we forget that God loves those with whom we argue,
that they are made in his image, and that Jesus died for them. This
is the necessary link between love of God and love of neighbor
for the sake of our love of God. The one is inextricably bound
to the other. When we act toward our neighbor in a way that is
contrary to charity, we undercut our love of God. At least we act
objectively contrary to the love of God. "He who does not love

his brother whom he has seen, cannot love God whom he has not seen" (I John 4:20).

The obligation to charity especially applies to loving the enemies of the faith and personal enemies we apologists have made. Jesus said, "Love your enemies and pray for those who persecute you" (Matt. 5:44). Loving our enemies does not necessarily mean liking them. We can distinguish feelings of affection from love. Feelings are one thing; acts of the will, another. We can love people without liking them and like people without loving them.

When we love an enemy in the sense to which Jesus refers, we desire his good and we will to do good to him. When it comes to apologetics, this includes respecting others as persons, beings of intellect and will. It means telling them the truth in love, in ways most suited to make them receptive to the truth and with the best arguments we can muster. It means respecting their freedom and trying to find as much to agree upon as possible before considering what we disagree about.

To paraphrase Paul in I Corinthians 13:4–7, charitable apologetics is patient and kind. It is not jealous or pompous or inflated or rude. It is not quick-tempered. It neither seeks its own interests nor broods over injury. Charitable apologetics rejoices not over wrongdoing, but in the truth. It bears all things, believes all things, hopes all things, endures all things.

In the final analysis, our love of God determines whether we are true apologists, not our love of arguments, our books, our audiotapes, or how many converts we have made. Arguments, books, audiotapes, and convert-making can be ways to express and strengthen our love of God, but they must never become a substitute for it.

Conclusion

We have discussed the Seven Deadly Sins of Catholic Apologetics and some of the habits we need to acquire in order to overcome those sins. Conquering sin is seldom easy. It requires commitment, struggle, and surrender to God. Most of all, it requires reliance on God's grace and mercy. Conquering the Seven Deadly Sins of Catholic Apologetics is not easy, but it is necessary if the much-needed apologetics revival the Holy Spirit has wrought is to bear all the fruit God desires. To that end, we apologists should examine our consciences, repent where necessary, develop the habits of effective apologists, and sincerely pray the words of the great Christian apologist C. S. Lewis:

> From all my lame defeats and oh! much more
> From all the victories that I seemed to score;
> From cleverness shot forth on Thy behalf
> At which, while angels weep, the audience laugh;
> From all my proofs of Thy divinity,
> Thou, who wouldst give no sign, deliver me.
>
> Thoughts are but coins. Let me not trust, instead
> Of Thee, their thin-worn image of Thy head.
> From all my thoughts, even from my thoughts of Thee
> O thou fair Silence, fall, and set me free.
> Lord of the narrow gate and the needle's eye,
> Take from me all my trumpery lest I die.

Recommended Reading

Adler, Mortimer J., *Truth in Religion*, New York: Macmillan Publishing Company, 1990

Ashley, O.P., Benedict M., *Choosing a World-View and Value-System*, New York: Alba House, 2000

Balthasar, Hans Urs von, *The Glory of the Lord*, vol. 1, San Francisco: Ignatius Press, 1982

Bouyer, Louis, *The Spirit and Forms of Protestantism*, Princeton, New Jersey: Scepter Publishing, 2001

D'Arcy, S.J., M.C., *The Nature of Belief*, St. Louis: B. Herder Book Co., 1958

De Broglie, S.J., Guy, *Revelation and Reason*, New York: Hawthorn Books, 1965

De Lubac, Henri, *The Christian Faith*, San Francisco: Ignatius Press, 1986

Derrick, Christopher, *That Strange Divine Sea*, San Francisco: Ignatius Press, 1985

Dubay, Thomas, *Faith and Certitude*, San Francisco: Ignatius Press, 1985

———, *The Evidential Power of Beauty*, San Francisco: Ignatius Press, 1999

Dulles, Avery, *The Assurance of Things Hoped For*, New York: Oxford University Press, 1994

———, *The Craft of Theology*, expanded edition, New York: Crossroad, 1995

Gilson, Étienne, *Reason and Revelation in the Middle Ages*, New York: Scribners, 1938

Kasper, Walter, *Transcending All Understanding*, San Francisco: Ignatius/Communio, 1989

Keating, Karl, *Catholicism and Fundamentalism*, San Francisco: Ignatius Press, 1988

——, *Controversies*, San Francisco: Ignatius Press, 2001

Knox, Ronald, *The Belief of Catholics*, San Francisco: Ignatius Press, 2000

Kreeft, Peter, *Ecumenical Jihad*, San Francisco: Ignatius Press, 1996

Kreeft, Peter, and Tacelli, Ronald, *Handbook of Christian Apologetics*, Downers Grove, Ill.: InterVarsity Press, 1994

Latourelle, S.J., Rene, *Theology: Science of Salvation*, New York: Alba House, 1969

Nichols, O.P., Aidan, *Catholic Thought Since the Enlightenment*, Leominster, England: Gracewing, 1998

——, *A Grammar of Consent*, Notre Dame, Ind.: University of Notre Dame Press, 1991

——, *The Shape of Catholic Theology*, Collegeville, Minn.: The Liturgical Press, 1991

Pieper, Josef, *Faith, Hope, Love*, San Francisco: Ignatius Press, 1997

Ratzinger, Joseph, *The Nature and Mission of Theology*, San Francisco: Ignatius Press, 1995

Sheed, Frank, *The Church and I*, Garden City, N.Y.: Doubleday & Company, 1974

——, *God and the Human Mind*, New York: Sheed and Ward, 1966

——, *Theology and Sanity*, San Francisco: Ignatius Press, 1993